Edwa

Chronicle

Cover image: Edward VI (c. 1550), by William Scrots
The Royal Collection

Contents

Preface 4

The *Chronicle* 8

Glossary 118

Key Figures 121

Preface

Despite dying at fifteen years of age and reigning for just six years, King Edward VI oversaw a dramatic, turbulent and deeply consequential period in English history. His time on the throne was marred by economic hardship, domestic unrest, costly foreign wars, factional strife and fierce opposition to the Protestant Reformation he championed. The two men who had the honour of leading his minority government lost their heads and the King's futile attempt at changing the line of succession on his deathbed almost resulted in civil war.

Thanks to his half-sister, Elizabeth I, Edward VI's religious legacy has endured into the present day, and his name has been immortalised in popular culture by Mark Twain's *The Prince and the Pauper*.

But who needs literature or intermediaries when you can hear all about this larger-than-life character first-hand – from the King himself?

As the sole male heir of England's most infamous king, Henry VIII, Edward benefitted from the best education money could buy. Skilled in multiple languages, he spent an extraordinary amount of time putting quill to parchment, gifting historians with a profusion of documentary evidence to feast their eyes on.

Out of all his writings, the *Chronicle* is far and away the most extensive and well-known. Technically, the work was untitled. Edward referred to it as his *Chronicle* on the page where the title of a work-in-progress was typically written, but later crossed it out.

Nevertheless, it is probably the best title on offer. Though some people prefer to call it a 'diary' this would be inaccurate, given that no such term existed at the time and the text recalled events – including those relating directly to Edward – in a distant, biographical manner.

The *Chronicle* begins with a brief record of his birth in October 1537 and progresses to discuss a range of political issues and events leading up to its abrupt termination on 28 November 1552 – some two months before the King fell fatally ill. He is believed to have started writing the work shortly after his coronation in February 1547, and it probably began as an educational exercise set by his tutors. This would explain why it initially reads like an outsider looking in – composed in the third person and defined by a stiff, formal manner.

From the spring of 1550, however, a marked shift can be observed within the text. Edward's writing becomes more detailed, sophisticated and informal, as well as broadening its spectrum of interest: focusing not just on the people and events immediately around the King, but on the broader issues of administration, finance and foreign affairs. It is significant that the years leading up to July 1550 account for just a quarter of the entire work and surely reflects the young king's growing role in political life. He was no longer a passive observer of the affairs of state he was describing. He was an active participant with an increasingly independent mind. And at the same time he started to make the *Chronicle* his own.

To say the least, Edward's *Chronicle* is a unique historical source. Part private diary, part educational exercise, part record of current affairs, few equivalents can be found in European history. Certainly it is one of the most important sources of information for the young king's short but eventful reign. After all, there are some instances of great consequence where it's the *only* source of information.

Nevertheless, the *Chronicle* should be treated with some caution. When read as a private diary rather than as the educational exercise it actually was, it gives the impression that Edward was a cold, harsh and callous individual. He recorded the execution of his uncle and Lord Protector in a single matter-of-fact sentence and failed to mention the death of his maternal grandmother at all. But that is not to say he lacked warmth or boyish affection, or that he did not love his family. It is important to remember that, as a king, he was rigorously trained to restrain his emotions – both in public and in private, as well as in person and on paper. Only rarely within the manuscript is the veil of disciplined regality drawn back in a burst of excitement and enthusiasm to give us an impression of the *real* Edward Tudor.

But these ambiguities, blank spaces and unanswered questions are not necessarily a bad thing. After all, it's the mysteries that make history fun in the first place. What Edward VI was like and to what extent he was a puppet of greedy and ambitious ministers continues to be a matter of heated scholarly debate – and it likely will be for many generations to come. Disagreement drives innovation. It makes people think. It allows them to look at the same old evidence with a new pair of eyes. And where evidence is insufficient, it motivates them to search for more.

B.R. Egginton
17 January 2021

The *Chronicle* today

The *Chronicle* manuscript is composed of sixty-eight pages and bound with a variety of other documents written by the King's hand. It was kept in the Royal Library until around 1616 when it fell into the hands of the renowned antiquarian Sir Robert Bruce Cotton. Benefitting from free access to state papers, Cotton acquired an extensive library of more than a hundred volumes of state documents during his busy life, almost all of which originated from the period 1509-1615.

In 1707 the contents of the Cotton Library were purchased by act of Parliament to serve as the basis of a national library, and the entire collection was absorbed by the British Museum upon its creation in 1753.

The *Chroncile* is now held in the British Library and can be found at: Cotton MSS., Nero, C, x.

Note on accuracy

Most entries within the *Chronicle* appear to have been penned on the date indicated. This assumption is based on the fact that Edward often had to correct or expand on the events and issues he discussed in later passages, as and when he received updates on current affairs. Some of the most notable errors are highlighted in the footnotes.

Alterations to manuscript

For ease of reading some changes have been made to the original text. The spellings and punctuation used by the young king has been modernised, and foreign place and family names have been anglicised. In the instances where archaic words have been retained, the glossary at the end of the book clarifies their meaning.

The *Chronicle*

The year of Our Lord 1537 was a prince born to King Harry the Eight[h] by Jane Seymour then Queen, who within [a] few days after the birth of her son died and was buried at the castle of Windsor. This child was christened by the Duke of Norfolk, the Duke of Suffolk, and the Archbishop of Canterbury. Afterward [he] was brought up, [un]til he came to six years old, among the women. At the sixth year of his age he was brought up in learning by Mr. Dr. [Richard] Cox, who was after[ward] his Almoner, and John Cheke, (Bachelor of Arts *crossed out*) Master of Arts, two well-learned men, who sought to bring him up in learning of tongues, of scripture, of philosophy, and all liberal sciences. Also John Belmaine, [a] Frenchman, did teach him the French language. The tenth year not yet (completed *crossed out*) ended, it was appointed he should be created Prince of Wales, Duke of Cornwall, and Count Palatine of Chester. At which time, being the year of Our Lord 1547, the said King died of a dropsy, as it was thought. After whose death incontinent, came Edward, Earl of Hertford, and Sir Anthony Browne, Master of the Horse, to convey this prince to Enfield, where the Earl of Hertford declared him and his younger sister Elizabeth the death of their father.

After the death of King Henry the Eighth, his son Edward, Prince of Wales, was come to at Hertford by the Earl of Hertford and Sir Anthony Browne, Master of the Horse, for whom before[hand] was made great preparation that he might [be] created Prince of Wales, and afterward was brought to Enfield, where the death of his father was first showed him, and the same day the death of his father was showed in London, where [there] was great lamentation and weeping; and suddenly he [was] proclaimed King. The next day, being the [31st] of [January] he was brought to the Tower of London, where he tarried the space of three weeks; and in the mean season the Council sat every day for the performance of the will and at length thought it best that the Earl of Hertford should be made Duke of Somerset, Sir Thomas Seymour Lord Sudeley, the Earl of Essex Marquis if Northampton, and divers (other *crossed out*) knights should be made barons, as the Lord Sheffield, with divers other[s]. Also they thought best to choose the Duke of Somerset to be Protector of the realm and Governor of the King's person (to which *crossed out*) during his minority, to which all the gentlemen and lords did agree, because he was the King's uncle on his mother's side. Also in this time the late King was buried at Windsor with much solemnity, and the officers broke their staves, hurling them into the grave. But they were restored to them again when they came to the Tower. The Lord Lisle was made Earl of Warwick, and the lord great chamberlainship was given to him; and the Lord Sudeley [was] made Admiral of England.

All those (this *in manuscript*) things were done, the King being in the Tower. Afterward, all things being prepared for the coronation, the King, being then but nine years old, passed through the City of London (and *crossed out*), as heretofore has been used, and came to the palace of Westminster, and the next day came into Westminster Hall, and it was asked [of] the people (whether they would have him to be their) King, who answered "Yea, yea." Then he was crowned King of England, France, and Ireland by the Archbishop of Canterbury and all the rest of the clergy and nobles, and anointed with all such ceremonies as were accustomed, and took his oath, and gave a general pardon, and so was brought to the hall to dinner, Shrove Sunday, where he sat with the crown on his head, with the Archbishop of Canterbury and the Lord Protector and all the Lords sat at boards in the hall beneath, and the Lord Marshal's deputy (for my Lord of Somerset was Lord Marshal) rode about the hall to make room. Then came in Sir John Dymoke, Champion, and made his challenge, and so the King drank to him and he had the cup. At night the King returned to his (hall *crossed out*) palace at Westminster, where there were jousts and barriers; and afterward order was taken for all his servants being with his father and [with] him [while] being prince, and the ordinary and unordinary were appointed.

In the mean season Sir Andrew Dudley, brother to my Lord of Warwick being in the "Pauncy," met with the "Lion," a principal ship of Scotland, which thought to take the "Pauncy" without resistance. But the "Pauncy" approached her and she shot, but at length they came very near, and then the "Pauncy," shooting off all one side, burst all the orlop (over love *in manuscript*) of the "Lion" and all her tackle, and at length boarded her and took her. But on the return, by negligence, she was lost at Harwich haven with almost all her men.

In the month of May died the French King, called Francis, and his son called Harry was proclaimed King.[1] There came also out of Scotland an ambassador, but [this] brought nothing to pass, and an army was prepared [to go] into Scotland.

Certain injunctions were set forth which took away divers ceremonies; and [a] commission [was] sent to take down images; and certain homilies were set forth to be read in the church.

Dr. Smith of Oxford recanted at [St] Paul's certain opinions of the mass and that Christ was not according to the order of Melchizedek.

The Lord Seymour of Sudeley married the Queen, whose name was Catherine, with which marriage the Lord Protector was much offended.

There was great preparation made to go into Scotland, and the Lord Protector, the Earl of Warwick, the Lord Dacre, the Lord Grey [of Wilton], and Mr. Bryan went with a great number of nobles and gentlemen to Berwick where, the first day after his coming, he mustered all his company, which were to the number of 13,000 footmen and 5,000 horsemen. The next day he marched on into Scotland and so passed the Path. Then he burned two castles in Scotland and so passed astraight of a bridge where 300 Scottish light horsemen set upon him behind him, who were discomfited. So he passed to Musselburgh, where the first day after he came he went up to the hill and saw the Scots, thinking them – as they were indeed – at the least (23,000 *crossed out*) 36,000 men, and my Lord of Warwick was almost taken, chasing the Earl of Huntly, by an

---

[1] This is an error: Francis I really died on 31 March 1547.

ambush. But he was rescued by one Berteville, with twelve harquebusiers on horseback, and the ambush ran away. The 7th day of September the Lord Protector thought to get the hill, which, the Scots seeing, passed the bridge over the river of Musselburgh, and strove for the higher ground and almost got it. But our horsemen set upon them, who, although they stayed them, yet were put to flight and gathered together again by the Duke of Somerset, Lord Protector, and the Earl of Warwick and were ready to give a new onset. The Scots, being amazed with this, fled their ways, some to Edinburgh, some to the sea[?], and some to Dalkeith, and there were slain 10,000 of them. But of Englishmen 51 horsemen, which were almost all gentlemen, and but one footman [were slain]. Prisoners were taken: the Lord Huntly, Chancellor of Scotland and divers other gentlemen, and [there were] slain of lords a thousand. And Mr. Bryan, Sadler, and Vane were made bannerets.[2]

After this battle Broughty [Castle] was given to the Englishmen, and Home and Roxburgh and Eyemouth, which were fortified, and captains were put in them; and the Lord of Somerset [was] rewarded with £500 [of] lands.

In the mean season Steph[en] Gardiner, Bishop of Winchester, was, for not receiving the injunctions, committed to ward.

There was also a Parliament called, wherein all chantries were granted to the King and an extreme law made for vagabonds, and divers other things.

Also the Scots besieged Broughty Castle, which was defended against them all by Sir Andrew Dudley, knight, and oftentimes their ordnance was taken and marred.

---

[2] With the exception of the casualty figures, Edward's account of the battle is remarkably accurate.

2nd Year

A triumph was, where six gentlemen did challenge all comers at barriers, jousts, and tourney; and also that they would keep a fortress with thirty with them, against a hundred or under, which was done at Greenwich.

Sir Edward Bellingham being sent into Ireland [as] Deputy, and Sir Anthony St. Leger revoked, he took O'Connor and O'More, bringing the lords that rebelled into subjection; and O'Connor and O'More, leaving their lordships, had apiece a hundred pound pension.

The Scots besieged the town of Haddington, where the captain Mr. Wilford every day made issues upon them and slew divers of them. The thing was very weak but for the men, who did very manfully. Oftentimes Mr. Holcroft and Mr. Palmer did victual it by force, passing through the enemies. And at the last the Rhinegrave unaware set upon Mr. Palmer, who (which *in manuscript*) was there with near[ly] a thousand and 500 horsemen, and discomforted him, taking him, Mr. Bowes, Warden of the West Marches, and divers other[s] to the number of 400, and slew a few.

(Upon St. Peter's day the Bishop of Winchester was committed to the Tower *added*.)

Then they made divers bragges[3], and they had [the] like made to them. Then went the Earl of Shrewsbury, General of the Army, with a [force of] 22,000 men and burned divers towns and fortresses, which, the Frenchmen and Scots hearing, levied their siege in the month of September; in the levying of which there came [some] to Tiberio, who as then was in Haddington and, setting forth the weakness of the town, told him that all honour was due to the defenders and none to the assailers; so the siege being levied, the Earl of Shrewsbury entered it and victualed and reinforced it. After his departing by night there came in to the outer court at Haddington 2,000 men, armed, taking the townsmen in

---

[3] 'Bragges' may mean 'brack', which is synonymous with 'breach'.

their shirts, which yet defended them with the help of the watch, and at length with ordnance issued out upon them and slew a marvellous number, bearing divers hot assaults, and at length driving[?] them home and kept the town safe.

A Parliament was called, where a uniform order of prayer was instituted, before made by a number of bishops and learned men gathered together in Windsor. There was granted a subsidy, and there was a notable disputation of the sacrament in the Parliament House.[4]

Also the Lord Sudeley, Admiral of England, was condemned to death and died the March ensuing. Sir Thomas Sharington was also condemned for making false coin, which he himself confessed; divers also were put in the Tower.

3rd Year

Home Castle was taken by night and treason by the Scots. Mr. Wilford in a skirmish was left of his men sore hurt and taken. There was a skirmish at Broughty Castle, wherein Mr. Luttrell, captain after Mr. Dudley, did burn certain villages and took Monsieur de Toge prisoner.

The Frenchmen by night (besieged *crossed out*) assaulted Bolemberg and were manfully repulsed. After[ward] they had made faggots with pitch, tar, tallow, rosin, powder, and wildfire, to burn the ships in the haven of Boulogne. But they were driven away by the Boulognois and their faggots taken.

In Mr. Bowes's place, who was Warden of the West Marches, was put the Lord Dacre; and in the Lord Grey's place the Earl of Rutland, who after his coming entered Scotland and burned divers villages and took much prey.

The people began to rise in Wiltshire, where Sir William Herbert did put them down, overrun, and slay them. Then they rose in Sussex,

---

[4] The last six words of this sentence are hard to determine.

Hampshire, Kent, Gloucestershire, Suffolk, Warwickshire, Essex, Hertfordshire, a piece of Leicestershire, Worcestershire, and Rutlandshire, where by fair persuasions, partly of honest men[?] among themselves and partly by gentlemen, they were often appeased, and again, because certain commissions were sent down to pluck down enclosures, then [they] did arise again.

The French King, perceiving this, caused war to be proclaimed and, hearing that our ships lay at Jersey, sent a great number of his galleys and certain ships to surprise our ships; but they, lying at anchor, beat the French [so] that they were fain to retire with a loss of a thousand of their men. At the same time the French King passed by Boulogne to Newhaven with his army and took Blackness by treason and the Almain camp; which done, Newhaven surrendered. There were also, in a skirmish between 300 English footmen and 700 French horsemen, six noblemen slain. Then the French King came with his army to Boulogne, which, they seeing, raised Bolemberg. But because of the plague he was compelled to retire, and Châtillon was left behind as governor of the army.

In the mean season, because there was a rumour that I was dead, I passed through London.

After that they rose in Oxfordshire, Devonshire, Norfolk, and Yorkshire.

To Oxfordshire the Lord Grey of Wilton was sent with 1,500 horsemen and footmen, whose coming, with the assembling of the gentlemen of the country, did so abash the rebels that more than half of them ran their ways, and [of the] other[s] that tarried were some slain, some taken, and some hanged.

To Devonshire the Lord Privy Seal was sent, who with his band, being but small, lay at Honiton while the rebels besieged Exeter, who did r[a]ise divers pretty feats of war. For after divers skirmishes, when the gates were burned, they in the city did continue the fire till they had made a rampart within. Also afterward, when they were undermined and power was laid in the mine, they within drowned the powder and the mine with water they cast in; which the Lord Privy Seal hearing, thought to have gone to reinforce them [by] a by-way; of which the rebels having spial [they] cut all the trees betwixt Ottery St. Mary and Exeter. For which cause the Lord Privy Seal burned that town and thought to return home. The rebels kept a bridge behind his back and so compelled him with his small band to set upon them, which he did and overcame them, killing 600 of them, and returning home without any loss of men. Then the Lord Grey and Spinola with their bands came to him, and afterward Grey with 200 of Reading, with which bands he, being reinforced, came to raise the siege at Exeter, forbecause they had scarcity of victuals; and as he passed from Honiton he came to a little town of his own, whither came but only two ways, which they had reinforced with two bulwarks made of earth and had put to the defence of the same about 2,000 men, and the rest they had laid: some at a bridge called Honiton bridge, partly at a certain hedge in a highway, and the most part at the siege of Exeter. The rearward of the horsemen, of which Travers was captain, set upon the one bulwark, the vanguard and battle on the other. Spinola's band kept them occupied at their wall. At length Travers drove them into town [Clyst St. Mary], which the Lord Privy Seal burned. Then they ran to a bridge nearby, from whence being driven, there were in a plain about 900 of them slain. The next day there were met about [an]other 2,000 of them at the entry of a highway, who first desired to talk and in the mean season fortified themselves, which being perceived, they ran their ways, and that same night the city of Exeter was delivered of the siege.

After that they gathered at Launceston, to whom the Lord Privy Seal and Sir William Herbert went, and overthrew them, taking their chief heads and executing them. Nevertheless, some sailed to Bridgwater and went about sedition but were quickly repressed. Hitherto of Devonshire.

At this time the "Black Galley" taken.[5]

---

[5] This brief statement probably refers to a ship seized by the French, following the outbreak of war between England and France on 8 August 1549.

Now to Norfolk. The people suddenly gathered together in Norfolk and increased to a great number, against whom was the Lord Marquis [of] Northampton sent with the number of 1,060 horsemen, who, winning the town of Norwich, kept it one day and one night, and the next day in the morning with loss of 100 men departed out of the town, among whom the Lord Sheffield was slain (taken prisoner *crossed out*). There were taken divers gentlemen and servingmen to the number of thirty, with which victory the rebels were very glad. But afterward, hearing that the Earl of Warwick came against them, they began to stay upon a strong plot of ground upon a hill near to the town of Norwich, having the town confederate with them. The Earl of Warwick came with the number of 6,000 men and 1,500 horsemen and entered into the town of Norwich, which having won, it was so weak that he could scarcely defend it, and oftentimes the rebels came into the streets killing divers of his men and were repulsed again, yea, and the townsmen were given to mischief themselves. So, having endured their assaults three days and stopped their victuals, the rebels were constrained for lack of meat to remove, whom the Earl of Warwick followed with 1,000 Almains and all his horsemen, leaving the English footmen in the town, and overcame them in plain battle, killing 2,000 of them and taking Kett their captain, who in January following was hanged at Norwich and his head hanged out. Kett's brother [William] was taken also and punished alike.

In the mean season Châtillon besieged the pier of Boulogne, [which had been] made in the haven, and after long battery of 20,000 shot or more gave assault to it and were manfully repulsed. Nevertheless they continued the siege still and made often skirmishes and false assaults in which they won not much. Therefore, seeing they profited little that way, they planted ordnance against the mouth of the haven, that no victuals might come to it, which our men seeing, [they] set upon them by night and slew divers Frenchmen and dismounted many of their pieces. Nevertheless, the French came another time and planted their ordnance toward the sand side on the sand hills and beat divers ships of victualers at the entry of the haven; but yet the Englishmen at the King's adventure came into the haven and refreshed divers times the town. The

Frenchmen, seeing they could not that way prevail, continued their battery but smally [*sic*], on which before they had spent 1,500 shot in a day, but loaded a gallery with stones and gravel which they let go in the stream to sink it, but or ere it sank it came near to one bank, where the Boulognois took it out and brought the stones to reinforce the pier.

Also at Guînes was a certain skirmish in which there was about a hundred Frenchmen slain, of which some were gentlemen and noblemen.

In the mean season in England rose great stirs, likely to increase much if it had not been well foreseen. The Council, about nineteen of them, were gathered in London, thinking to meet with the Lord Protector and to make him amend some of his disorders. He, fearing his state, caused the Secretary in my name to be sent to the Lords to know for what cause they gathered their powers together and, if they meant to talk with him, [to say] that they should come in peaceable manner. The next morning, being the 6th of October, and Saturday, he commanded the armour to be brought down out of the armoury of Hampton Court, about 500 harnesses, to arm both his and my men withal, the gates of the house to be rempared, [and] people to be raised. People came abundantly to the house. That night, with all the people, at nine or ten o'clock at night, I went to Windsor, and there was watch and ward kept every night. The Lords sat in [the] open places of London, calling for gentlemen before them and declaring the causes of accusation of the Lord Protector, and caused the same to be proclaimed. After which time few came to Windsor but only mine own men of the guard, whom the Lords willed, fearing the rage of the people so lately quieted. Then began the Protector to treat by letters, sending Sir Philip Hoby, lately come from his embassy in Flanders to see to his family, who brought on his return a letter to the Protector very gentle, which he delivered to him, another to me, another to my house, to declare his faults, ambition, vainglory, entering into rash wars in mine youth, negligent looking on Newhaven, enriching of himself of my treasure, following his own opinion, and doing all by his own authority, etc.; which letters were openly read, and immediately the Lords came to Windsor, took him, and brought him through Holborn to the Tower. Afterward I came to Hampton Court, where they appointed by my consent six Lords of the Council to be attendant on me, at least two, and four knights; Lords: the Marquis [of] Northampton, the Earls of Warwick and Arundel, Lords Russell, St. John, and Wentworth; knights: Sir Andrew Dudley, Sir Edward Rogers, Sir Thomas Darcy, Sir Thomas Wroth. After[ward] I came through London to Westminster. The Lord of Warwick [was] made Admiral of England. Sir Thomas Cheyney [was] sent to the Emperor for relief, which he could not obtain. Mr. [Nicholas] Wotton [was] made Secretary. The Lord Protector, by his own agreement and submission, lost his protectorship, treasurership, marshalship, all his moveables, and near[ly] £2,000 [of] lands, by act of Parliament.

The Earl of Arundel committed to his house for certain crimes of suspicion against him, as plucking down of bolts and locks at Westminster, giving of my stuff away, etc., and put to fine of £12,000, to be paid £1,000 yearly; of which he was after[ward] released.

PART OF THE CHRONICLE 3 ANNO REG. REGIS E. SEXT. IN CHARTA 1549

Also Mr. Southwell committed to the Tower for certain bills of sedition written with his hand and put to [a] fine of £500. Likewise Sir Thomas Arundel and Sir John committed to the Tower for conspiracies in the west[ern] parts.

A parliament, where was made a manner to consecrate priests, bishops, and deacons.

Mr. Paget, surrendering his comptrollership, was made Lord Paget of Beaudesert and cited into the higher house by a writ of Parliament.

Sir Anthony Wingfield, before Vice-Chamberlain, made Comptroller. Sir Thomas Darcy made Vice-Chamberlain.

I passed through London the 15th of October. At Hampton Court the Lord of Warwick made Lord Admiral.[6]

Guidotti made divers errands from the Constable of France to make peace with us, upon which were appointed four commissioners to treat, and they after long debatement made a treaty as followeth: [*The rest of the page (and maybe more) is missing.*]

AN. D'NI 1549 [1550] – MARCH

24. Peace concluded between England, France, and Scotland by, on the English side, John Earl of Bedford, Lord Privy Seal; Lord Paget de Beaudesert; Sir William Petre, Secretary; and Sir John Mason; on the French side, Monsieur de Rochepot, Mons. Châtillon, Guillart de Mortier, and Bochetel de Sassy, upon condition that all titles, tributes, and defences should remain; that the fault of one man, except he be unpunished, should not break the league; that the ships of merchandise shall pass to and fro, that pirates shall be called back, and ships of war; that prisoners shall be delivered of both sides; that we shall not war with Scotland, except new occasion be given; that Boulogne, with the pieces of new conquest, and two basilisks, two demicannon, three culverins, two demiculverins, three sakers, six[teen?] falcons, ninety-four harquebuses a croc with wooden tails, twenty-one iron pieces; and Lauder and Dunglass, with all the ordnance, save that that came from Haddington, shall within six months after this peace [is] proclaimed be delivered; and for the French: to pay 200,000 scutes within three days after the delivery of Boulogne, and 200,000 scutes on Our Lady's Day in [the] harvest next ensuing, and that if the Scots razed Lauder, etc., we should raze Roxburgh and Eyemouth. For the performance of which on the 7th of April should be delivered at Guînes and Ardres these hostages:

Marquis de Mayenne	My Lord Suffolk
Mons. Trémoille	My Lord of Hertford

---

[6] Part of this is crossed out, and it is also out of place chronologically.

Mons. D'Enghein	My Lord Talbot
Mons. De Montmorency	My Lord FitzWarren
Mons. De la Hunaudaye	My Lord Maltravers
Vidame de Chartres	My Lord Strange

Also that at the delivery of the town ours should come home, and at the first payment three of theirs; and that if the Scots raze Lauder and Dunglass we must raze Eyemouth and Roxburgh, and no one[?] after[ward] fortify there. With comprehension of the Emperor.

AN. D'NI 1550

25. This peace proclaimed at Calais and Boulogne.

29. In London. Bonfires.

30. A Sermon in thanksgiving for peace, and *Te Deum* sung.

31. My Lord Somerset was (delivered [of] his bonds) and came to court.[7]

1550 – APRIL

2. The Parliament [in] April prorogued to the second day of the term in October next ensuing.

3. Nicholas Ridley, before of Rochester, made Bishop of London and received his oath.
Thomas Thirlby, before of Westminster, made Bishop of Norwich and received his oath.

5. The Bishop of Chichester, before a vehement affirmer of transubstantiation, did preach against [it] at Westminster in the preaching place.
Removing to Greenwich from Westminster.

6. Our hostages passed the Narrow Seas between Dover and Calais.

---

[7] The manuscript is frayed and torn here, and the exact wording is unclear.

7. Mons. De F[umel], gentleman of the King's Privy Chamber, passed from the French King by England to the Scottish Queen to tell her of the peace.
An ambassador came from Gustavus the Sweden King, called Andre, for a surer amity touching merchandises.

9. The hostages [were] delivered on both sides for the ratification of the league with France and Scotland, forbecause some[one] said to Mons. Rochepot, lieutenant, that Mons. de Guise, father to the Marquis de Mayenne, was dead, and therefore the delivery was put over a day.

8. My Lord Warwick made general Warden of the North, and Mr. Herbert President of Wales; and the one had granted to him a thousand marks [worth] of land, the other five hundred, and Lord Warwick 100 horsemen at my (*altered to* King charge).

9. Licensers signed for the whole Council and certain of the Privy Chamber to keep among them (*altered to* 2,290) 2,340 retainers.

10. My Lord Somerset taken into the Council. Guidotti, the beginner of the talk for peace, recompensed with knightdom, a thousand crowns (pound *crossed out*) reward, a thousand crowns pension, and his son with 250 crowns (pound *crossed out*) pension. Certain prisoners for light matters dismissed. Agreed for delivery of French prisoners taken in the wars. Peter Vannes sent [as] ambassador to Venice. Letters directed to certain nobles to take a blind legate (bishop c*rossed out*) coming from the Pope calling himself Bishop of Armagh. Commissions for the delivery of Boulogne, Lauder, and Dunglass.

6. Three Flemish men-of-war would have passed our ships without vailing bonnet, which they seeing shot at them and drove them at length to vail bonnet and so depart.

11. Mons. Trémoille, Mons. Vidame de Chartres, and Mons. Hunaudaye came to Dover; the rest tarried at Calais till they have leave.

12. Order taken that whosoever had benefices given them should preach before the King in or out of Lent, and [that] every Sunday there should be a sermon.

16. The three hostages aforesaid came to London, being met at Deptford by the Lord Grey of Wilton, Lord Braye, with divers other gentlemen to the number of twenty, and servingmen one hundred, and so brought into the City and lodged there and kept [in] houses – every man by himself.

18. Mr. Sidney and Mr. Neville made gentlemen of the Privy Chamber. Commission given to the Lord Cobham, Deputy of Calais; Sir William Petre, Chief Secretary; and Sir John Mason, French Secretary, to see the French King take his oath, with certain instructions; and that Sir John Mason should be ambassador ledger.
Commission to Sir John [Maurice] Dennis and Sir William Sharington to receive the first payment and deliver the quittance.

10. Sir John Mason taken into the Privy Council and William Thomas made clerk of the same.
Whereas the Emperor's ambassador desired leave by letters patent that my Lady Mary might have (leave to say *crossed out*) mass, it was denied him; and when[?] he said we broke the league with him by making peace with Scotland, it was answered that the French King and not I did comprehend them, saving that I might not invade them without occasion.

10. Lauder being besieged of the Scots, the captain, hearing that the peace was proclaimed in England, delivered it, as the peace did will him, taking sureties that all the bargains of the peace should be kept.

18. Monsieur de Guise died.

20. Order taken for the Chamber that three of the outer Privy Chamber gentlemen should always be here, and two lie in the palat[8] and fill the room of one of the four knights; that the esquires should be diligent in

---

[8] 'Palat' presumably means 'pallet'. This was a small bed, typically laid directly on the floor.

their office, and five grooms should be always present of which one to watch in the bedchamber.

21. The Marquis de Mayenne, the Duc d'Enghien, and the Constable's son arrived at Dover.

23. Mons. de la Trémoille and the Vidame of Chartres and Mons. Hunaudaye came to the court and saw the Order of the Garter and the knights with the sovereign receive the communion.

24. Certain articles touching a straiter amity in merchandise sent to the King of Sweden, being these: First, if the King of Sweden sends bullion, he should have our commodities and pay no toll. Secondly, he should bring bullion to no other prince.
Thirdly, if he brought osmunds and steel and copper, etc., he should have our commodities and pay custom as an Englishman. Fourthly, if he brought any other he should have free intercourse, paying custom as a stranger, etc.
It was answered to the Duke of Brunswick [Brandenburg] that whereas he offered service with 10,000 men of his band, that the war was ended; and [as] for the marriage of my Lady Mary to him, there was talk for her marriage with the Infante of Portugal, which being determined, he should have answer.[9]

25. The Lord Clinton, captain of Boulogne, having sent away before[hand] all his men saving 1,800 and all his ordnance saving that [which] the treaty did reserve, issued out of the town with these 1,800, delivering it to Mons. Châtillon, receiving of him the six hostages English, a quittance for delivery of the town, and safe-conduct to come to Calais, whither when he came he placed 1,800 on the Emperor's frontiers.

---

[9] Here Edward mistakenly states that the suit was proposed by the Duke of Brunswick.

27. The Marquis de Mayenne, Count d'Enghein, and the Constable's son were received at Blackheath by my Lord of Rutland, my Lord Grey of Wilton, my Lord Braye, my Lord Lisle, and divers gentlemen, with all the pensioners to the number of 100, beside a great number of servingmen.

It was granted that my Lord of Somerset should have all his moveable goods and leases except those that be already given.

The King of Sweden's ambassador departed home to his master.

29. The Court d'Enghien, brother to the Duke of Vendôme and next heir to the crown after the King's children, the Marquis de Mayenne, brother of the Scottish Queen, and Mons. Montmoreney, the Constable's son, came to the court, where they were received with much music at dinner.

26. Certain [ones] were taken that went about to have an insurrection in Kent upon May Day following, and the priest who was the chief worker ran away into Essex, where he was laid for.

30. Dunglass was delivered, as the treaty did require.

MAY

2. Joan Bocher, otherwise called Joan of Kent, was burned for holding that Christ was not incarnate of the Virgin Mary, being condemned the year before but kept in hope of conversion; and the 30th of April the Bishop of London and the Bishop of Ely were to persuade her. But she withstood them and reviled the preacher that preached at her death.

The first payment was paid at Calais and received by Sir Thomas [Maurice] Dennis and Mr. Sharington.

4. The Lord Clinton, before captain of Boulogne, came to the court, where, after thanks, he was made Admiral of England, upon the surrender of the Earl of Warwick's patent. He was also taken into the Privy Council and promised further reward. The captains also and officers of the town were promised rewards. Mons. de Brézé also passed by the court [en route] to Scotland, where at Greenwich he came to the

King, telling him that the French King would see that if he lacked any commodity that he had, he would give it [to] him and likewise would the Constable of France, who then bore all the suing.

5. The Marquis of Mayenne departed into Scotland with Mons. de Brézé to comfort the Queen of the death of the Duke of Guise.
The Master of Erskine and Mons. Morette's brother came out of Scotland for the acceptance of the peace, who after[ward] had passport to go into France.

7. The Council drew [up] a book for every shire, who should be lieutenants in them and who should tarry with me; but the lieutenants were appointed to tarry till Châtillon's, Sassy's, and Bochetel's coming and then to depart.

9. Proclamation was made that the soldiers should return to their mansions, and the Mayor of London had charge to look through all the wards, to take them and send them to their countries.
The debt of £30,000 and odd money was put over a year, and there was bought 2,500 quintals of powder.

11. Proclamation was made that all wool-winders should take (have *crossed out*) an oath that they would make good cloth there as the Lord Chancellor would appoint them according to an act of Parliament made by Edward the Third.

7. The Lord Cobham, the Secretary Petre, and Sir John Mason came to the French King to Amiens, going on his journey, where they were received of all the nobles and so brought to their lodgings, which were well dressed.

12. Our ambassadors departed from the French court, leaving Sir John Mason as ledger.

14. The Duke of Somerset was taken into the Privy Chamber, and likewise was the Lord Admiral [Clinton].

15. It was appointed that all the light horsemen of Boulogne and the men of arms should be paid their wages and be led by the Lord Marquis of Northampton, captain of the pensionaries, and all the guard of Boulogne under the Lord Admiral. Also that the chiefest captains should be sent with 600 with them to the strengthening of the frontiers of Scotland.

The (making *crossed out*) comprehension of peace with Scotland was accepted so far as the league went and sealed with the [*sentence unfinished*].

16. The Master of Erskine departed into France.

(17. The French King came to Boulogne. Removing from Greenwich *crossed out*.)

17. Removing to Westminster from Greenwich.

18. The French King came to Boulogne to visit the pieces lately delivered to him and to appoint an order and stay in things there, which done, he departed.

19. Peter Vannes went as ambassador to Venice and departed from the court with his instructions.

20. The Lord Cobham and Sir William Petre came home from their journey, delivering both the oath, the testimonial of the oath witnessed by divers noblemen of France, and also the treaty, sealed with the great seal of France; and in the oath was confessed that I was Supreme Head of the Church of England and Ireland, and also King of Ireland.

23. Mons. Châtillon and Mortier and Bochetel, accompanied with the Rhinegrave d'Andelot, the Constable's second son, and Chemault the ledger, came to Durham Place, where in their journey they were met by Mr. Treasurer [Cheyney] and threescore gentlemen at Woolwich and also saluted with great peals both at Woolwich, Deptford, and the Tower.

24. The ambassadors came to me, presenting the ledger, and also delivering letters of credence from the French King.

25. The ambassadors came to the court, where they saw me take the oath for the acceptance of the treaty, and afterward dined with me; and after dinner saw a pastime of ten against ten at the ring, whereof on the one side were the Duke of Suffolk, the Vidame [of Chartres], the Lord Lisle, and seven other gentlemen apparelled in yellow; on the other, the Lord Strange, Mons. Hunaudaye, and eight others, in blue.

26. The ambassadors saw the baiting of the bears and bulls.

27. The ambassadors, after they had hunted, sat with me at supper.

28. The same went to see Hampton Court, where they did hunt and the same night return to Durham Place.

25. One that, by way of (have *in manuscript*) marriage, had thought to assemble the people and so make an insurrection in Kent, was taken by the gentlemen of the shire and afterward punished.

29. The ambassadors had a fair supper made them by the Duke of Somerset and afterward went into the Thames and saw both the bear hunted in the river and also wildfire[?] cast out of boats, and many pretty conceits.

30. The ambassadors took their leave and the next day departed.

JUNE

3. The King came to Sheen, where was a marriage made between the Lord Lisle, the Earl of Warwick's son, and the Lady Anne, daughter to the Duke of Somerset, which done and a fair dinner made and dancing finished, the King and the ladies went into two chambers made of boughs, where first he [the King] saw six gentlemen of one side and six of another run the course of the field, twice over. Their names here do follow:

The Lord Edward [Seymour]. Sir John Appleby. [*The rest of the names are omitted, although space was left for them to be filled in.*]
And afterward came three masquers of one side and two of another, which ran four courses apiece. Their names be [*blank*].
Last of all came the Count of Rangone, with three Italians, who ran with all the gentlemen four courses and afterward fought at tourney. And so after supper he (the King) returned to Westminster.[10]

4. Sir Robert Dudley, third[11] son to the Earl of Warwick, married Sir John Robsart's daughter, after which marriage there were certain gentlemen that did strive who should first take away a goose's head which was hanged alive on two cross posts.

5. There was tilt and tourney on foot with as great staves as they [could] run withal on horseback.

6. Removing to Greenwich.

8. The gests of my progress were set forth, which were these: from Greenwich to Westminster, from Westminster to Hampton Court, from Hampton Court to Windsor, from Windsor to Guildford, from Guildford to Oatlands, from Oatlands to Richmond, etc.
Also Vidame made a great supper to the Duke of Somerset and the Marquis of Northampton, with divers masques and other conceits.

9. The Duke of Somerset, Marquis [of] Northampton, Lord Treasurer, [the Earl of] Bedford, and the Secretary Petre went to the Bishop of Winchester to know to what he would stick, he made answer that he would obey and set forth all things set forth by me and my Parliament; and if he were troubled in conscience he would reveal it to the Council and not reason openly against it. (Also... *crossed out*)
The first payment of the French men was laid up in the Tower for all chances.

---

[10] The manuscript is badly frayed here. There might be another word or two following 'to'.
[11] This should be 'fifth'.

10. The books of my proceedings was sent to the Bishop of Winchester to see whether he would set his hand to it or promise to set it forth to the people.

11. Order was given for fortifying and victualing Calais for four months; and also Sir Harry Palmer and Sir [Richard] Lee were sent to the frontiers of Scotland to take a view of all the forts there and to report to the Council where they thought best to fortify. There was also sent to Alderney [John] Rogers and [Thomas] Atwood to make fortifications there.

12. The Marquis de Mayenne came from Scotland in post and went his way into France.

13. Commissions were signed to Sir William Herbert and thirty others to entreat of certain matters in Wales, and also instructions to the same how to behave himself in the presidentship.

14. The surveyor of Calais was sent to Calais, first to raise the walls of Risebank toward the sand hills and after[ward] to make the wall massy again, and the round bulwark to [be] change[d] to a pointed one which should run 26 feet into the sea to bear the sand hills, and to raise the mount. Secondly, to Newnhambridge to make a high bulwark in the midst, with flankers to beat through all the strait and also four sluices to make Calais haven better. Afterward he was bid to go to Guînes, where first he should take away the four-cornered bulwark to make the outward wall of the keep, and to fill the space between the keep and the said outward wall with the aforesaid bulwark, and to raise the old keep that it might beat[?] the town[?]. Also he was bid to make Purton's bulwark where it is now round without flankers both pointed, and also with six flankers to bear hard to the keep.
Atwood and [Thomas] Lambert were sent to take view of Alderney, Scilly, Jersey, Guernsey, and the Isle of Jethou.
The Duke of Somerset, with five others of the Council, went to the Bishop of Winchester, to whom he made this answer: "I having deliberately seen the Book of Common Prayer, although I would not

have made it so myself, yet I find such things in it as satisfy my conscience and therefore both I will execute it myself and also see other my parishioners to do it." This was subscribed by the aforesaid Councillors, that they heard him saying these words.

16. The Lord Marquis [of Northampton], Mr. Herbert, the Vidame, Hunaudaye, and divers other gentlemen went to the Earl of Warwick's, where they were honourably received, and the next day there ran at the ring a great number of gentlemen.

19. I went to Deptford, being bidden to supper by the Lord Clinton, where before supper I saw certain [men] stand upon the end of a boat without hold of anything and ran one at another until one was cast into the water. At supper Mons. Vidame and Hunaudaye supped with me. After supper was there a fort made upon a great lighter on the Thames, which had three walls and a watchtower in the midst, of which Mr. Winter was captain, with forty or fifty other soldiers in yellow and black. To the fort also appertained a galley of yellow colour with men and munition in it for defence of the castle. Wherefore there came four pinnaces with their men in white handsomely dressed, which, intending to give assault to the castle, first drove away the yellow pinnace, and after[ward] with clods, squibs, canes of fire, darts made for the nonce, and bombards [they] assaulted the castle; and at length [they] came with their pieces and burst the outer walls of the castle, beating them of the castle into the second ward, who after[ward] issued out and drove away the pinnaces, sinking one of them, out of which all the men in it, being more than twenty, leaped out and swam in the Thames. Then came the Admiral of the Navy with three other pinnaces and won the castle by assault and burst the top of it down and took the captain and under-captain. Then the Admiral went forth to take the yellow ship and at length clasped with her, took her, and assaulted her top, and won it by composition and so returned home.

20. The Mayor of London caused the watches to be increased every night because of the great frays, and also one alderman to see good rule kept every night.

22. There was a privy search made through all Sussex for all vagabonds, gypsies, conspirators, prophets, ill players, and suchlike.

24. There were certain [men who] in Essex about Romford went about a conspiracy, which were taken and the matter stayed.

25. Removing to Greenwich.

23. Sir John Gates, Sheriff of Essex, went down with letters to see the Bishop of London's injunctions performed, which touched plucking down of superaltars, altars, and suchlike ceremonies and abuses.

29. It was appointed that the Germans should have the Austin Friars for their church to have their service in, for avoiding of all sects of Anabaptists and suchlike.

17. The French Queen was delivered of a third son, called Mons. d'Angoulême.

13. The Emperor departed from Argentina [Strassburg] to Augusta [Augsburg].

30. John Ponet made Bishop of Rochester and received his oath.

JULY

5. There was money provided to be sent into Ireland for payment of the soldiers there, and also order taken for the dispatch of the strangers in London.

7. The Master of Erskine passed into Scotland, coming from France. Also the French ambassador did come before me, first, after showing the birth of Mons. d'Angoulême, afterward declaring that, whereas the

French King had for my sake let go the prisoners at St. Andrew's, who before they were taken had shamefully murdered the Cardinal, he desired that all Scots that were prisoners [should be released]; it was answered that all were delivered. Then he moved for one called the Archbishop of Glasgow, who since the peace came disguised without passport and so was taken; it was answered that we had no peace with Scotland such that they might pass [through] our country, and the Master of Erskine affirmed the same.

8. It was agreed that the two hundred that were with me, and two hundred with Mr. Herbert, should be sent into Ireland. Also that the mint should be set awork that it might win £24,000 a year and so bear all my charges and Ireland for this year, and [add] £10,000 to my coffers.

9. The Earl of Warwick, the Lord Treasurer, Sir William Herbert, and the Secretary Petre went to the Bishop of Winchester with certain articles signed by me and the Council, containing the confessing of his fault: the supremacy, the establishing of holy days, the abolishing of [the] six articles, and divers other, whereof the copy is in the Council chest, whereunto he put his hand, save (saving *in manuscript*) to the confession.

10. Sir William Herbert and the Secretary Petre were sent unto him to tell him I marveled that he would not put his hand to the confession; to whom he made answer that he would not put his hand to the confession forbecause he was innocent; and also the confession was but the preface of the articles.

11. The Bishop of London, the Secretary Petre, Mr. Cecil, and Goodrich were commanded to make certain articles according to the laws and to put them in the submission.

12. It was appointed that under the shadow of preparing for the same[?] (ea *in manuscript*) matters there should be sent £5,000 to the Protestants to get their good will.

14. The Bishop of Winchester did deny the articles that the Bishop of London and the other had made.

13. Sir John Gates sent into Essex to stop the going away of the Lady Mary, because it was credibly informed that Scepperus should steal her away to Antwerp, divers of her gentlemen were there, and Scepperus a little before came to see the landing places.

16. It was appointed that the two hundred with the Duke of Somerset and two hundred with the Lord Privy Seal and four hundred with Mr. St. Leger should be sent to the seacoast.

17. It was agreed that on Wednesday next we should go in one day to Windsor and dine at Sion.

18. It was thought best that the Lord Bowes should tarry in his wardenship still, and the Earl of Warwick should tarry here and be recompensed.

19. The Bishop of Winchester was sequestered from his fruits for three months.

20. Hooper was made Bishop of Gloucester. The merchants were commanded to stay as much as they could their vent into Flanders because the Emperor had made many strait laws against them that professed the Gospel.

21. A muster was made of the Boulognois, who were wholly paid for all past and a month to come.
Sir John Wallop, Francis Hall, and Doctor Cook were appointed commissioners to appoint the limits between me and the French King.

23. Removing to Windsor.

22. The Secretary Petre and [the] Lord Chancellor were appointed to go to the Lady Mary to cause her to come to Woking or to the court.

25. It was appointed that half the French King's first payment should be bestowed on paying £10,000 at Calais, £9,000 in Ireland, £16,000 in the North, 2,000 in the Admiralty, so that every crown might go for one of our nobles.

27. Because the rumour came so much of Scepperus' coming, it was appointed that they of the Admiralty should set my ships in readiness.

26. The Duke of Somerset went to set order in Oxfordshire, Sussex, Wiltshire, and Hampshire.

28. The Lady Mary after long communication was content to come to Leighs to the Lord Chancellor and then to Hunsdon, but she utterly denied to come to the court or Woking at that time.

31. The Earl of Southampton died.

14. Andrea Doria took the city of Africa [Mehedia] from the pirate Dragut, who in the mean season burned the country of Genoa.

8. The Emperor came to Augsburg.

AUGUST

4. Mr. St. Leger was appointed by my letters patent to be deputy there [in Ireland] and had his commission, instructions, and letters to the nobles of Ireland for the same purpose.

5. The same deputy departed from the castle of Windsor.

6. The Duke of Somerset departed to Reading to take an order there.

7. It was appointed that of the money delivered to me by the French King there should be taken 100,000 crowns: to pay 10,000 pounds at Calais, [15],000 in the North and 2,000 in the Admiralty and 8,000 in Ireland.

8. Mons. Hunaudaye took his leave to depart to Calais and so upon the payment to be delivered home; and Trémoille, being sick, went in a horse-litter to Dover.

9. The French ambassador came to Windsor to sue for passport for the Dowager of Scotland, which being granted so she came like a friend, he required 300 horse to pass with 200 keepers, which was not wholly granted, but only that 200 horse with 150 keepers in one company, coming into this realm as should be appointed, should without let pass into France and not return this way.

11. The Vidame of Chartres showed his license to tarry here and a letter written to the same purpose.

10. The ambassador of France departed, not a little contented with his gentle answers.

12. Removing to Guildford.

13. The Parliament was prorogued to the 20th of February next following. Mr. Cook, Master of Requests, and certain other lawyers were appointed to make a short table of the laws and acts that were not wholly unprofitable and to present it to the board.

1[3?] The Lord Chancellor fell sore sick, with forty more of his horse, so that the Lady Mary came not thither at that time.

14. There came divers advertisements from [Sir Thomas] Chamberlain, ambassador with the Queen of Hungary, that their very intent was to take away the Lady Mary and so to begin an outward war and an inward conspiracy, insomuch that the Queen said Scepperus was but a coward and, for fear of one gentleman that came down, durst not go forth with his enterprise to my Lady Mary.

16. The Earl of Maxwell came down to the north borders with a good power to overthrow Grahams, who were a certain family that were yielded to me. But the Lord Dacre stood before his face with a good

band of men and so put him from his purpose, and the gentlemen called Grahams skirmished with the said Earl, slaying certain of his men.

17. The Council appointed among themselves that none of them should speak in any man's behalf for land to be given, reversion of offices, leases of manors, or extraordinary annuities, except for certain captains who served at Boulogne, their answer being deferred to Michaelmas next.

18. A proclamation that until Michaelmas all strangers that sued for pensions should go their way.

20. Removing to Woking.

15. The second payment of the French was paid and Hunaudaye and Trémoille delivered.

21. Eight thousand pounds of the last payment was appointed to be paid to the dispatch of Calais, and 5,000 to (at *in manuscript*) the North.

24. Ten thousand [pounds] was appointed to be occupied to win money to pay the next year [for] the outward pay[?], and it was promised that the money should double every month.

20. Removing to Oatlands.

27. Andrea Doria gave a hot assault to the town of Africa, kept by the pirate called Dragut Arraiz, but was repulsed by the townsmen.

29. The pirate gave a hot assault to Andrea Doria by night and slew the captain of Tunis, with divers other notable men.

31. The Duke Maurice [of Saxony] made answer to the Emperor that if the Council were not free he would not come to (at *in manuscript*) it.

SEPTEMBER

2. Maclamore in Ireland, before a rebel, by the means of Mr. Brabazon surrendered himself and gave pledges.

6. Mr. Wotton gave up his secretaryship, and Mr. Cecil (took it.)[12]

SEPTEMBER A D'NI 1550, 2 CHARTA

8. Removing to Nonesuch.

15. Removing to Oatlands.

22. A proclamation was set forth by the which it was commanded, first, that no kind of victual, no wax, tallow candles, not no such thing should be carried over except to Calais, putting in sureties to go thither. Secondarily, that no man should buy or sell the selfsame things again, except brokers, who should not have more than ten quarters of grain at once. Thirdly, that all justices should divide themselves into hundreds, rapes, and wapentakes, to look in their quarters [to see] what superfluous corn were in every barn and appoint it to be sold at a reasonable price. Also that one of them must be in every market to see the corn brought. Furthermore, whosoever shipped over anything aforesaid to the parties of beyond sea or [to] Scotland after eight days following the publication of the proclamation should forfeit his ship and the ware[s] therein, half to the lord of the franchise and half to the finder thereof. Whoso bought to sell again after the day aforesaid should forfeit all his goods, farms, and leases to the use one half of the finder, the other of the King. Whoso brought not in corn to the market as he was appointed should forfeit ten pounds, except the purveyors took it up or it was sold to his neighbours.

25. Letters sent out to the justices of [the] peace for the due execution thereof.

---

[12] Manuscript frayed. Exact wording uncertain.

18. Andrea Doria had a repulse from the town of Africa and lost many of his men and the captain of Tunis and nevertheless left not yet the siege.

24. Order was given for the victualing of Calais.

26. The Lord Willoughby, Deputy of Calais, departed and took his journey thitherward.

28. The Lord Treasurer [Paulet] sent to London to give order for the preservation of the City with the help of the Mayor.

15. Whereas the Emperor required a Council, they were content to receive it so it were free and ordinary, requiring also that every man might be restored to his right and a general peace proclaimed. They desired also that in the mean season no man might be restrained to use his [the Emperor's] fashion of religion.

18. The Emperor made answer that the Council should be to the glory of God and maintenance of the empire, at Trent. He knew no title to any of his territories. Peace he desired and in the mean season would have them observe the Interim and [the] last Council of Trent; he would also that they of Bremen and Hamburg, with their associates, should leave their seditions and obey his decrees.

21. George, Duke of Mecklenburg, came with 8,000 men of war to the city of Magdeburg, being Protestant, against whom went forth the Count of Mansfeld and his brother with 6,000 men and eight guns, to drive him from pillage. But the other, abiding the battle, put the Count to flight, took his brother prisoner, and slew 3,000 men, as it is reported.

OCTOBER

4. Removing to Richmond.

5. The Parliament prorogued to the twentieth of January.

6. The French King made his entry into Rouen.

10. It was agreed that [Sir John] York, master of one of the mints at the Tower, should make this bargain with me, viz.: To make the profit of (my *crossed out*) silver rising of the bullion that he himself brought, [he] should pay all my debts, to the sum of £1,200,000[13] or above, and remain accountable for the overplus, paying no more but 6*s*. and 6*d*. the ounce, till the exchange were equal in Flanders, and after[ward] 6*s*. and 2*d*. Also that he should declare all his bargains to any [who] should be appointed for to oversee him and leave off when I would. For which I should give him £15,000 in prest-[money] and leave to carry £8,000 overseas to abase the exchange.

16. Removing to Westminster.

19. Pieces were set on (of *in manuscript*) all kind of grains, butter, cheese, and poultry ware by a proclamation.

20. The Frenchmen came to Sandingfield and Fiennes-wood to the number of 800 and there on my ground did spoil my subjects that were relieved by the wood.

26. The French ambassador came to excuse the aforesaid men, saying they thought it not meet that that wood should be spoiled of us, being thought and claimed as theirs, and therefore they lay there.

24. There were 1,000 men embarked to go to Calais, and so to Guînes and Hammes, Risebank, Newnhambridge, the Cause[wa]y, and the bulwarks, with victuals for the same.

NOVEMBER

19. There were letters sent to every bishop to pluck down the altars.

---

[13] The correct figure was £120,000.

20. There were letters sent down to the gentlemen of every shire for the observation of the last proclamation touching corn, because there came none to the markets – commanding them to punish the offenders.

29. Upon the letters written back by the same, the proclamation was abolished.

DECEMBER

15. There were (was *in manuscript*) letters sent for the taking of certain chaplains of the Lady Mary for saying mass, which she denied.

19. Borthwick was sent to the King of Denmark with privy instructions for marriage of the Lady Elizabeth to his son.

20. There was appointed a band of horsemen divided amongst the nobles, a hundred to the Duke of Somerset. Fifty [each] to my Lord Marquis North[ampton], to the Earl of Warwick, Lord Privy Seal, Mr. Herbert, Mr. Treasurer (To the Lord Treasurer *crossed out*). Lord Ma[rquis] Dorset, Earl of Wilt[shire], Lord Wentworth, Lord Admiral, Lord Paget, Mr. Sadler, Mr. Darcy.

21. Removing to Greenwich.

26. Peace concluded between the Emperor and the Scots.

JANUARY [1551]

6. The Earl of Arundel remitted of £8,000 which he ought to have paid for certain faults he had committed within twelve years.

7. There was appointed, forbecause the Frenchmen did go about practice in Ireland, that there should be prepared four ships, four barks, four pinnaces, and twelve victualers to take three havens, of which two were on the south side toward France and one in James Carr's the Scot's country, and also to send and break the aforesaid conspiracies.

10. Three ships, being sent forth into the Narrow Seas, took certain pirates and brought them into England, where the most part [of them] was hanged.

27. Mons. de Lansac came from the French King by way of request to ask that Cawe Mills, the fishing of the Tweed, Edrington, the Ground [De]batable, and the Scottish hostages that were put here in the King's my father's days should be delivered to the Scots; that they might be suffered to traffic as though they were in peace, and that all interest of the aforesaid houses [hostages?] should be delivered to the Scots. Also that those prisoners which were bound to pay their ransoms before the peace (their departure *crossed out*) last concluded should not enjoy the benefit of the peace.

18. The Lord Cobham was appointed to be general lieutenant of Ireland.

30. Letters written to Mr. St. Leger to repair the south[ern] parts of Ireland with his force.

FEBRUARY

3. Mr. Croft appointed to go into Ireland and there with [John] Rogers and certain artificers to take the havens aforesaid and begin some fortifications.

5. Divers merchants of London were spoken withal for provision of corn out of Denmark, about 40,000 quarters.

10. Mountford was commanded to go to provide for certain preparations of victuals for the ships that should go into Ireland.

11. Also for provision to be sent to Berwick and the north parts.

16. Whalley was examined for persuading divers nobles of the realm to make the Duke of Somerset Protector at the next Parliament and stood to the denial, the Earl of Rutland affirming it manifestly.

13. The Bishop of Winchester, after a long trial, was deposed of his bishopric.

20. Sir William Pickering, knight, was dispatched to the French King for answer to Mons. de Lansac, to declare that, although I had [the] right in the aforesaid places yet I was content to forbear them under conditions to be agreed on by commissioners on both sides, and [that] for the last article I agreed without condition.

25. The Lord Marquis Dorset appointed to be Warden of the North Borders, having three sub-wardens, the Lord Ogle [in the Middle March], and Sir [Nicholas Stelley] in the East, and the Lord [John] Conyers in the West.
Also Mr. Aucher had the charge for victualing of Calais.

28. The learned man Bucer died at Cambridge, who was two days after[ward] buried in St. Marys' Church at Cambridge, all the whole university with the whole town bringing him to the grave, to the number [of] 3,000 persons; also there was an oration of Mr. Haddon made very eloquently at his death and a sermon of [Dr. Matthew Parker]. After that Mr. Redman made a third sermon. Which three sermons made the people wonderfully to lament his death. Last of all, all the learned men of the university made their epitaphs in his praise, laying them on his grave.

MARCH

3. The Lord Wentworth, Lord Chamberlain, died about ten of the clock at night, leaving behind him sixteen children.

8. Sir John York had great loss, about £2,000 worth[?] of silver, by treason of Englishmen, which he brought for provision of the mints. Also [Sir Andrew] Judd 1,500; also Tresham [Sir John Gresham] 500, so the whole came to £4,000.

FEBRUARY

20. The Frenchmen came with a navy of 160 sails into Scotland, laden with provision of grain, powder, and ordnance, of which sixteen great ships perished on Ireland['s] coast, two laden with artillery and fourteen with corn. Also in this month the Deputy there set at one certain of the west lords that were at variance.

MARCH

10. Certain new fortifications were devised to be made at Calais, [so] that at Gravelines the water should be let in in my ground and so should fett a compass by the six bulwarks to Guînes, Hammes, and Newnhambridge, and that there should be a wall of 8 foot high and 6 broad of earth to keep out the water, and to make a great marsh about the territory of Calais 37 miles long. Also for flankers at the keep of Guînes [are] willed to be made, a three-cornered bulwark at the keep, to keep it. Furthermore, at Newnhambridge a massy wall to the French side there as was agreed. Besides, at the west jetty there should be another jetty which should defend the victualers of the town always from shot from the sandhills.

5. Mr. Aucher had £2,000 in money, wherewith he provided out of Flanders for Calais 2,000 quarters of barley [and] 500 of wheat.

18. The Lady Mary, my sister, came to me to Westminster, where after salutations she was called with my Council into a chamber where was declared how long I had suffered her mass (against my will *crossed out*) in hope of her reconciliation and how now, being no hope, which I perceived by her letters, except I saw some short amendment, I could not bear it. She answered that her soul was God['s] and her faith she would not change, nor dissemble her opinion with contrary doings. It was said I constrained not her faith but willed her (not as a king to rule *added*) but as a subject to obey. And that her example might breed too much inconvenience.

19. The Emperor's ambassador came with [a] short message from his master of [threatened] war, [to know] if I would not suffer his cousin the princess to use her mass. To this was no answer given at this time (but at the next *crossed out*).

20. The Bis[hops] of Canterbury, London, [and] Rochester did conclude [that] to give license to sin was sin; to suffer and wink at it for a time might be borne, so all haste possible might be used.

23. The Council, having the Bishops' answers, seeing [that] my subjects, lacking their vent in Flanders, might put the whole realm in danger; [that] the Flemings had cloth enough for a year in their hand and were kept far under; the danger of the Papists, the 1,500 quintals of powder I had in Flanders, the harness they had for preparation for the gendarmerie, the goods my merchants had there at the wool fleet, [they] decreed to send an ambassador to the Emperor, Mr. [Nicholas] Wotton, to deny the matter wholly and persuade the Emperor in it, thinking by his going to win some time for a preparation of a mart, conveyance of powder, harness, etc., and for the surety of the realm. In the mean season to punish the offenders, first, of my servants that heard mass, next, of hers.

22. Sir Anthony Browne sent to the Fleet for hearing mass, with Sergeant Morgan, Sir Clement Smith, which a year before heard mass, chided.

25. The ambassador of the Emperor came to have his answer but had none save that [some]one should go to the Emperor within a month or two to declare this matter.

22. Sir William Pickering came with great thanks from the French King.

27. Removing to Greenwich.

31. A challenge made by me that I, with sixteen of my chamber, should run at base, shoot, and run at ring with any seventeen of my servants,

gentlemen in the court.

Mr. Croft arrived in Ireland and came to Waterford to the Deputy consulting for fortification of the town.

APRIL

1. The first day of the challenge at base, or running, the King won.

3. Mons. de Lansac came again from the French King to go to Scotland for appointing of his commissioners on the Scottish side, who were: the French ambassador in Scotland, the Bishop [of Orkney or of Ross], the Master of Erskine, and [*sentence unfinished*].

5. Sir Thomas Darcy made Lord Darcy of Chiche and Lord Chamberlain, for the maintenance whereof he had given him 100 marks to his heirs general and 300 to his heirs male.

6. I lost the challenge of shooting at rounds and won at rovers.

7. There were appointed commissioners on my side: either the Bishop of Lichfield, if he had no impediment, or [of] Norwich, Mr. Bowes, Mr. Beckwith, and Sir Thomas Chaloner.

8. Sir John Gates made Vice-Chamberlain and captain of the guard, and had 120 pound[s worth of] land.

9. Ponet, Bishop of Rochester, received his oath for the bishopric of Winchester, having 2,000 marks [worth of] land appointed to him for his maintenance.

7. A certain Aryan of the Strangers, a Dutchman, being excommunicated by the congregation of his countrymen, was after long disputation condemned to the fire.

9. The Earl of Wiltshire had fifty more [men-at-arms] in my Lord Marquis Dorset's place, [now become] Warden of the North, and my Lord of Rutland in my Lord Wentworth's place [an]other fifty.

10. Mr. Wotton had his instructions made to go withal to the Emperor to be as ambassador ledger in Mr. Morison's place and to declare this resolution: that if the Emperor would suffer my ambassador with him to use his service, then I would his; if he would not suffer mine, I would not suffer his. Likewise that my sister was my subject and should use my service appointed by act of Parliament.

Also it was appointed to make twenty thousand pound weight for necessity somewhat baser, [in order] to get gains [of] £160,000 clear, by which the debt of the realm might be paid, the country defended from any sudden attempt, and the coin amended.

11. Mr. Pickering had his instructions and dispatch to go into France as ambassador ledger there in Mr. Mason's place, who desired very much to come home, and Mr. Pickering had instructions to tell the French King of the appointing of my commissioners in Scotland aforesaid.

12. They of Magdeburg, having in January last past taken in a conflict the Duke of Mecklenburg and three other earls, did give an onset on Duke Maurice by boats on the river when it overflowed the country, and slew divers of his men and came home safe, receiving a great portion of victuals into the town.

15. A conspiracy opened of the Essex men who within three days after minded to declare the coming of strangers and so to bring people together to Chelmsford and then to spoil the rich men's houses if they could. Woodcock!

16. Also [a conspiracy] of Londoners who thought to rise on May Day against the strangers of the City; and both the parties committed to ward.

23. This day the French King and the Lord Clinton chosen into the Order of the Garter, and appointed that Duke of Somerset, the Marquis of Northampton, the Earl of Wiltshire, and the Earl of Warwick should peruse and amend the Order.

PART OF APRIL, A 1551, 3 CHARTA, 5 REGNI E. 6

24. The Lords sat at London and banqueted one another this day and [for] three days after, for to show agreement amongst them whereas discord was bruited, and somewhat to look to the punishment of talebearers and apprehending of evil persons.

25. A bargain made with the Fuggers for about £60,000 that in May and August should be paid, for the deferring of it. First, that the Fuggers should put it off for ten in the hundred. Secondly, that I should buy 12,000 mark weight at six shillings the ounce, to be delivered at Antwerp and so conveyed over. Thirdly, I should pay 100,000 crowns for a very fair jewel of his, four rubies marvellous big, one orient and great diamond, and one great pearl.

27. Mallett, the Lady Mary's chaplain, apprehended and sent to the Tower of London.

30. The Lord Marquis [of] Northampton appointed to go with the Order and further commission of treaty and that in post, having joined with him in commission the Bishop of Ely, Sir Philip Hoby, Sir William Pickering, and Sir John Mason, knights, and two other lawyers: Smith that was Secretary and [Dr. John Oliver].

MAY

2. There was appointed to go with my Lord Marquis the Earls of Rutland, Worcester, and Ormonde, the Lords Lisle, Fitzwalter, and Braye, Abergavenny, and Evre, and divers other gentlemen to the number of (*altered to* twenty) 30 in all.

3. The challenge at running at ring performed, at the which first came the King, sixteen footmen, and ten horsemen, in black silk coats pulled out with white silk taffeta; then all lords having three[?] men likewise apparelled, and all gentlemen, their footmen in white fustian pulled out with black taffeta. The other side came all in yellow taffeta. At length

the yellow band took it twice in 120 courses, and my band tainted often – which was counted as nothing – and took never – which seemed very strange – and so the prize was of my side lost. After that, tourney followed between six of my band and six of theirs.

4. It was appointed that there should be but four men to wait on every earl that went with my Lord Marquis [of] Northampton, three on every lord, two on every knight or gentleman; also that my Lord Marquis should in his diet be allowed for the loss in his exchange.

5. The muster of the gendarmery appointed to be the first of June if it were possible; if not, the 8th.

6. The teston cried down from 12d. to 10d. and the groat from 4d. to 3d.

9. One [Robert] Stuart, a Scotsman, meaning to poison the young Queen of Scotland, thinking thereby to get favour here, was, after he had been a while in the Tower and Newgate, delivered on my frontiers at Calais to the French, for to have him punished there according to his deserts.

10. Divers lords and knights sent for to furnish the court at the coming of the French ambassador that brought hither the Order of St. Michael.

12. A proclamation proclaimed to give warning to all those that keep many farms, multitudes of sheep above the number limited in the law, viz., 2,000, decay[ed] tenements and towns, regraters, forestallers, men that sell dear, having plenty enough, and put plow ground to pasture, and carriers over sea of victuals, that if they leave not these enormities they shall be straitly punished very shortly, so that they should feel the smart of it; and to command execution of laws made for these purposes before.

(14. The Earl of Warwick made–, *uncompleted entry crossed out.*)

14. There mustered before me 100 archers, two arrows apiece, all of the guard, [who] afterward shot together, and they shot at an inch board, which some pierced quite a stuck in the other board; divers pierced it quite through with the heads of their arrows, the boards being very well

seasoned timber. So it was appointed there should be ordinary 100 archers and 100 halberdiers, either good wrestlers or casters of the bar, or leapers, runners, or tall men of personage.

15. Sir Philip Hoby departed toward France with ten gentlemen of his own, in velvet coats and chains of gold.

16. Likewise did the Bishop of Ely depart with a band of men well-furnished.

20. A proclamation made that whosoever found a seditious bill and did not tear and deface it should be partaker of the bill and punished as the maker.

21. My Lord Marquis [of] Northampton had commission to deliver the Order [of the Garter] and to treat of all things, and chiefly of marriage for me to the Lady Elizabeth, his daughter: first, to have the dot 12,000 marks a year and the dowry at least 800,000 crowns. The forfeiture 100,000 crowns at the most, if I performed not; and paying that to be delivered. And that this should not impeach the former covenants with Scotland; with many other branches.

22. He departed himself in post.

24. An earthquake was at Croydon and Bletchingley and in the most part of Surrey, but no harm was done.

30. Whereas before commandment was given that £160,000 should be coined of 3 ounces in the pound fine for discharge of debts, and to get some treasure to be able to alter all, now was it stopped, saving only £80,000 to discharge my debts and 10,000 mark weight that the Fuggers delivered in the last exchange at 4 ounces in the pound.

31. The musters deferred till after midsummer.

JUNE

2. It was appointed that I should receive the Frenchmen that came hither at Westminster, where was made preparation for the purpose, and four garnish of new vessels prepared, taking out of church stuff, [such] as miters and golden missals and primers and crosses and relics of Plessay.

4. Provision made in Flanders for silver and gold plate and chains to be given to these strangers.

7. A proclamation set forth that exchanging or rechanging should be made under the punishment set forth in King Henry the 7.['s] time, duly to be executed.

10. Mons. Maréchal departed (out of Fra– *crossed out*) from the [French] court to Boulogne in post and so hither by water in his galleys and foists.
In this month and the month before was great business for the city of Parma, which Duke Horatio [Ottavio] had delivered to the French King. For the Pope accited him as holding it *in capite* of him, whereby he could not alienate it without the Pope's will; but he came not at his day, for which cause the Pope and [the] Imperials raised 3,000 men and took a castle on the same river side. Also the French King sent Mons. de Thermes, who had been his general in Scotland, with a great piece of his gendarmery into Italy to help Duke Horatio [Ottavio]. Furthermore, the Turk made great preparations for war, which some feared would at length burst out.

3. I was elected of the company of St. Michael in France, by the French King and his Order.

13. Agreement made with the Scots for the borders, between the commissioners aforesaid for both the parties.
In this month [Arraiz] Dragut, a pirate, escaped Andrea Doria, who had closed him in a creek, by force of his galley slaves that digged another

50

way into the sea and took two of Andrea's galleys that lay far into the sea.

14. Pardon given to those Irish lords that would come in before a certain day, limited by the Deputy, with advertisement to the Deputy to make sharp war with those that would resist, and also should minister my laws everywhere.

18. Because of my charges in fortifications at Calais and Berwick [that] should be paid, it was agreed that, besides the debt of the realm, £80,000[14], there should be £40,000 coined, three ounces fine [and] nine of alloy, and 5,000 pound weight should be coined in a standard of seven ounces fine, at the least.

17. Superantio [Giacomo Soranzo] came as ambassador from Venice in Daniel Barbaro's place.

16. I accepted the Order of St. Michael by promise to the French ambassador.

17. My Lord Marquis [of] North[ampton] came to Nantes with the commissioners and all the noblemen and gentlemen that came over sea with him.

20. Upon advertisement of Scepperus' coming and rigging of certain ships in Holland, also for to show the Frenchmen pleasure at their coming, all the navy that lay in Gillingham water was appointed to be rigged and furnished with ordnance and lie in the river of Thames, to the intent that if Scepperus came afterward he might be met with, and [that] at least the Frenchmen should see the force of my navy.

22. The Lady Mary sent letters to the Council, marvelling at the imprisonment of Doctor Mallett, her chaplain, for saying of the mass before her household, seeing it was promised the Emperor's ambassador

---

[14] This figure is hard to read and could alternatively be £60,000.

she should not be molested in religion, but that she and her household should have the mass said before them continually.

24. They [the Council] answered that because of their duties to their king, country, and friends, they were compelled to give her answer that they would see not only him but also other mass-sayers and breakers of order straitly punished, and that as for promise they had nor would give none to make her free from the punishment of the law in that behalf.

18. Châtillon came to my Lord Marquis [of Northampton] and there banqueted him by the way, at two times, between Nantes and Chateaubriant, where the King lay.

15. Mandosse, a gentleman of the King's chamber, was sent to him to conduct him to the court.

19. My Lord Marquis came to Chateaubriant, where half a mile from the castle there met him [the Comte d'Enghien and the Duc de Montpensier] with one hundred gentlemen and brought him to the court, and so, booted and spurred, to the French King.

20. The French King was invested with the Order of the Garter in his bedchamber, where he gave a chain to Garter worth £200 and his gown dressed with aglets worth £25. The Bishop of Ely making an oration and the Cardinal of Lorraine making him answer.
At afternoon the Lord Marquis moved the French King to the marriage of the Scottish Queen to be consummated, whose hearing he appointed to the commissioners.

21. The Cardinal[s] of Lorraine and of Châtillon, the Constable, [and] the Duke of Guise were appointed commissioners on the part of France, who absolutely denied the first motion for the Scottish Queen, saying both they had taken too much pain and spent too many lives for her, also a conclusion was made for her marriage to the Dauphin. Then was proposed the marriage of the Lady Elizabeth, the French King's eldest daughter, to which they did most cheerfully assent. So after they agreed

neither party to be bound in conscience nor honour until she was twelve years of age and upwards. Then they came to the dot, which was first asked 1,500,000 scutes of France, at which they made a mock. After, for *donatio propter nuptias*, the[y] agreed that it should be as great as hath been given by the King my father to any wife he had.

22. Our commissioners came to 1,400,000 of crowns, which they refused; then to a million, which they denied; then to 800,000 crowns, which they said they would not agree to.

23. Then our commissioners asked what they would offer. First they offered 100,000 crowns, then 200,000, which they said was the most and more than ever was given. Then followed great reasonings and showings of precedent, but no nearer they could come.

24. They went forward to the penalty if the parties misliked [one another] after that the King's daughter was twelve and upwards, which the French offered 100,000, 50,000 crowns, or promise. Then, that she should be brought at her father's charge three months before she was twelve, sufficiently jeweled and stuffed. Then bonds to be delivered alternatively at London and Paris, and so forth.

26. The Frenchmen delivered the aforesaid answers written to my commissioners.

JULY

1. Whereas certain Flemish ships, twelve sail in all, six tall men-of-war, looking for eighteen more of men-of-war, went to Dieppe, as it was thought, to take Mons. le Maréchal [St. André] by the way, order was given that six ships, being before prepared, with four pinnaces and a brigantine, should go both to conduct him and also to defend if anything should be attempted against England by carrying over the Lady Mary.

2. A brigantine sent (ship sent *crossed out*) to Dieppe to give knowledge to Mons. le Maréchal of the Flemings' coming, to whom all the

Flemings vailed their bonnet. Also the French ambassador was advertised; who answered that he thought him sure enough when he came into our streams – terming it so.

2. There was a proclamation signed for shortening of the fall of the money to that day in which it should be proclaimed, and [it was] devised that it should be in all places of the realm within one day proclaimed.

3. The Lords Clinton (and Cobham *crossed out*) were appointed to meet the French[man] at (*altered to* Woolwich) Gravesend and so to convey him to Durham Place, where he should lie.

4. I was banqueted by the Lord Clinton at Deptford, where I saw the "Primrose" and the "Mary Willoughby" launched.
The Frenchman landed at Rye, as some thought for fear of the Flemings lying at the land's end, chiefly because they saw out ships were let by the wind [so] that they could not come out.

6. Sir Pe[ter] Meutas at Dover was commanded to come to Rye to meet Mons. le Maréchal, who so did, and after he had delivered his letters, written with mine own hand, and made my recommendations, he took order for horses and carts for Mons. le Maréchal in which he made such provision as was possible (meet *crossed out*) to be for the sudden.

7. Mons. le Maréchal set forth from Rye, and in his journey Mr. Culpepper, [*blank space*], and divers other gentlemen, and their men, to the number of 1,000 horse well-furnished, met him and so brought him to Maidstone that night.
Removing to Westminster.

8. Mons. le Maréchal came to Mr. Baker's, where he was very well feasted and banqueted.

9. The same came to my Lord Cobham's to dinner and at night to Gravesend.
Proclamation made that a teston should go at 9*d.* and a groat at 3*d.* in all

places of the realm at once.
At this time came the sweat into London, which was more vehement than the old sweat. For if one took cold, he died within three hours, and if he escaped, it held him but nine hours, or ten at most. Also, if he slept the first six hours, as he should be very desirous to do, then he raved and should die raving.

11. It grew so much – for in London the tenth there died seventy in the liberties, and this day 120, (that I did remove *crossed out*) and also one of my gentlemen, another of my grooms, fell sick and died – that I removed to Hampton Court with very few with me.
The same night the Maréchal, who was saluted with all my ships being in the Thames, fifty and odd, all with shot well furnished and so with the ordnance of the Tower. He was met by the Lord Clinton, Lord Admiral, with forty gentlemen at Gravesend, and so brought to Durham Place.

13. Because of the infection at London, he came this day to Richmond, where he lay with a great band of gentlemen, at least 400, as it was by divers esteemed, where that night he hunted.

14. He came to me at Hampton Court at nine of the clock, being met by the Duke of Somerset at the wall end and so conveyed first to me, where, after his master's recommendations and letters, he went to his chamber on the Queen's side, all hanged with cloth of arras, and so was the hall and all my lodging. He dined with me also. After dinner, being brought into an inner chamber, he told me he was come not only for delivery of the Order but also for to declare the great friendship the King his master bore me, which he desired I would think to be such to me as a father beareth to his son, or brother to brother. And although there were divers persuasions, as he thought, to dissuade me from the King his master's friendship, and witless men made divers rumours, yet he trusted I would not believe them. Furthermore [he declared] that, as good ministers on the frontiers do great good, so do ill [ministers] much harm. For which cause he desired no innovation should be made on things [which] had been so long in controversy by handstrokes, but rather by

commissioners' talk. I answered him that I thanked him for his Order and also his love, etc., and I would show like love in all points. For rumours, they were not always to be believed; and that I did sometime provide for the worst but never did any harm upon their hearing. For ministers, I said I would rather appease these controversies with words than do anything by force. So after[ward] he was conveyed to Richmond again.

16. He came to present the Order of [St.] Michael; where, after with ceremonies accustomed he had put on the garments, he and Mons. Gyé, likewise of the Order, came – one at my right hand, the other at my left – to the chapel where, after the communion [was] celebrated, each of them kissed my cheek. After[ward] they dined with me and talked after dinner and saw some pastime and so went home again.

18. A proclamation made against regraters and forestallers, and the words of the statute recited, with the punishment for the offenders. Also letters were sent to all officers and sheriffs for the executing thereof.

19. Another proclamation made for punishment of them that would blow rumours of abasing and enhancing of the coin to make things dear withal.
The same night Mons. le Maréchal St. André supped with me; after supper saw a dozen courses, and after[ward] came and made me ready.

20. The next morning he came to see mine arraying and saw my bedchamber and went a-hunting with hounds and saw me shoot and saw all my guard shoot together. He dined with me, heard me play on the lute, ride [rode?], came to me in my study, supped with me, and so departed to Richmond.

19. The Scots sent an ambassador hither for receiving the treaty, sealed with the Great Seal of England, which was delivered [to] him. Also I sent Sir Thomas Chaloner, Clerk of my Council, to have the seal of them for confirmation of the last treaty at Norham.
This day my Lord Marquis [of Northampton] and the commissioners,

coming to treat of the marriage, offered by later instructions 600,000 crowns, after[ward] 400,000 s[cutes], and so departed for an hour. Then, seeing they could get no better, [they] came to the French offer of 200,000 s[cutes], half to be paid at the marriage, half six months after that. Then the French agreed that her dot should be but 10,000 marks of lawful money of England. Thirdly, it was agreed that if I died she[?] should[?] not have the dot, saying they did that for friendship's sake without precedent.

19. The Lord Marquis, having received and delivered again the treaty sealed, took his leave, and so did all the rest.
At this time was there a bickering at Parma between the French and the Papists. For Mons. de Thermes, Pietro Strozzi, and Fontanello, with divers other gentlemen to the number of thirty, with 1,500 soldiers, entered Parma. Gonzaga with the Emperor's and Pope's band lay near the town. The French made sallies and overcame [them], slaying the Prince of Macedonia and il signor Battista, the Pope's nephew.[15]

22. Mr. Sidney made one of the four chief gentlemen.

23. Mons. le Maréchal came to me, declaring the King his master's well-taking [of] my readiness to this treaty, and also how much his master was bent that way. He presented Mons. Boisdauphin to be ambassador here, as my Lord Marquis the 19th day did present Mr. Pickering.

26. Mons. le Maréchal dined with me; after dinner saw the strength of the English archers. After he had so done, at his departure I gave him a diamond from my finger worth by estimation £150 both for [his] pains and also for my memory. Then he took his leave.

27. He came to me a-hunting to tell me the news and show the letter his master had sent him, and doubles of Mons. Thermes' letter and Marillac's letters, [he] being ambassador with the Emperor.

---

[15] The report was incorrect. Giovanni Battista del Monte did not die until 14 April 1552.

28. Mons. le Maréchal cane to dinner to Hyde Park, where there was a fair house made for him, and he saw the coursing there.

30. He came to the Earl of Warwick's, lay there one night, and was well received.

29. He had his reward, being worth three thousand pounds in gold of current money, Mons. de Gyé £1,000, Mons. Chemault £1,000, Mons. Morvilliers 500, the secretary 500, and the Bishop [of] Périgueux 500.

AUGUST

3. Mons. le Maréchal departed to Boulogne and had certain of my ships to conduct him thither.

9. Twenty-four Lord of the Council met at Richmond to commune of my sister Mary's matter – who at length agreed that it was not meet to be suffered any longer, making thereof an instrument signed with their hands and sealed, to be of record.

11. The Lord Marquis with the most part of his band came home and delivered the treaty, sealed.

12. Letters sent for Rochester, Englefield, Waldegrave, etc., to come the seventeenth day, but they came not until another letter was sent to them the thirteenth day.

14. My Lord Marquis' reward was delivered at Paris, worth £500, my Lord of Ely's 200, Mr. Hoby's 150, the rest all about one scantling.

14. Rochester, etc., had commandment neither to hear nor to suffer any kind of service but the communion and orders set forth alar [at large?] by Parliament, and had one[?] letter to my Lady's house from my Council for their credit, another to her self from me. Also appointed that I should come to, and sit at, Council, when great matters were in debating, or when[?] I would.

This last month M. de Thermes with 500 Frenchmen came to Parma and

58

entered safely. Afterward certain issued out of the town and were overthrown, as M. Sipier, d'Andelot, Petro Corso, and others were taken and some slain. After they gave a skirmish, [they] entered the camp of Gonzaga and spoiled a few tents and returned.

15. Sir Robert Dudley and Barnaby [Fitzpatrick] sworn two of the six ordinary gentlemen.
The last month the Turks' navy won a little castle in Sicily.

17. Instructions sent to Sir James Croft [as Lord Deputy in Ireland] for divers purposes, whose copy is in the Secretary's hands.

18. The teston cried down from ninepence to sixpence, the groat from threepence to twopence, the twopence to a penny, the penny to a halfpenny, the halfpenny to a farthing, etc.
M. de Thermes and [M.] Sipier overthrew three ensigns of horsemen at three times, took one dispatch sent from Don Fernando [di Gonzaga] to the Pope concerning this war, and another from the Pope to Don Fernando, discomfited four ensigns of footmen, and took the Count Camillio [di Gonzaga] of Castiglione, and slew a captain of the Spaniards.

22. Removing to Windsor.

23. Rochester, etc., returned, denying to do openly the charge of the Lady Mary's house for displeasing her (here *in manuscript*).

26. The Lord Chancellor, Mr. Comptroller, and the Secretary Petre sent to do the same commission.

27. Mr. Coverdale made Bishop of Exeter.

28. Rochester, etc., sent to the Fleet.
The Lord Chancellor, etc., did that they were commanded to do to my sister and her house.

31. Rochester, etc., committed to the Tower.

The Duke of Somerset, taking certain that [there] began a new conspiracy for destruction of the gentlemen at Wokingham two days past, executed them with death for their offense.

29. Certain pinnaces were prepared to see that there should be no conveyance overseas of the lady Mary secretly done. Also appointed that the Lord Chancellor, the Lord Chamberlain, the Vice-Chamberlain, and the Secretary Petre should see by all means they could whether she used the mass, and if she did that the laws should be executed on her chaplains. Also that when I came from this progress to Hampton Court, or Westminster, both my sisters should be with me till further order were taken for this purpose.

SEPTEMBER A D'NI 1551, 4 CHARTA, 5 REGNI E. 6

3. The French ambassador came to declare, first, who [how] the Emperor wronged divers of his mater's subjects and vassals, arrested also his merchants, and did cloakedly begin war. For he besieged Mirandola round about with forts he had made in the French King's country. Also he stayed certain ships (of war *crossed out*) French going a-fishing to the Newfoundland. Furthermore, he sent a dozen ships which bragged they would take the Dowager of Scotland, which thing stayed her so long at Dieppe. Whereupon his master had taken the hool [wool] fleet of Antwerp, conveying it to his country into his ports by a ten ships he had sent forth under Baron de la Garde. Also minded to send more help to Piedmont and Mirandola. For this cause he desired that on my coasts the Dowager might have safe passage and might be succored with my servants at the seacoast if any chance should happen. He was willed to put it in writing. He showed how the Turks' navy, having spoiled a piece of Sicily, went to Malta and there took an isle adjacent called Gozo; from thence they went to Tripoli. In Transylvania, Rusta Bassa was leader of the army and had spoiled it wholly. In Hungary the Turks had made a fort by the miners to get them.

Magdeburg was freshly victualed, and Duke Maurice came his way, [it] being suspected he had conspired with them there.

4. It was answered to the French ambass[ador] that the Dowager should[?] in all my ports be defended from enemies [and] tempest, and likewise[?] also thanks were given for the news.

5. The Emperor's ambassador came to require that my sister[?] Mary's[?] officers should be restored to their liberty and [that] she should have[?] her[?] mass till the Emperor was certified thereof. It was answered, first, that I needed not to answer except I list, because he spoke without commission, which was seen by the shortness of the time since the committing of her officers, of which the Emperor could not be advertised. He was willed no more to move these piques, in which he had been often answered, without commission. He was answered that the Emperor was by this time advertised, although the matter pertained not to him. also, that I had done nothing but according to a king's office herein, in observing the laws that were so godly and in punishing the offenders. The promise to the Emperor was not so made as he pretended, [as is] affirmed by Sir Philip Hoby, being at that [time] there [the] ambassador.

6. Deliberation touching the coin. Memor. that there were divers standards – 9 ounces fine a few; 8 ounces fine as ill as four, because although that that [*sic*] was fine, yet a shilling was reckoned for two shillings; 6 ounces, very many; 4 ounces, many also; 3 ounces £130,000 now of late. Whereupon agreed that the teston being called to sixpence, 4 with help of 6 should make ten fine, 8 fine with help of nine, being fewer than those of eight, should make ten ounces fine; the two ounces of alloy should quit the charges of minting; and those of threepence, being but few, should be turned to [the stan]dard of 4, of farthings and halfpence and pence for to serve for the poor people, because [the mer]chants made no exchange of it and the sum was not great; also to [bear the] charges, forbecause it was thought that few or none were left of 9 ounces fine, 8 ounces were nought, and 6 ounces were two ways

devised, one without any craft, the other was not fully six – of which kind was not a few.

9. A proclamation set forth touching the pieces of cattle, of hogs, pigs, beefs, oxen, mutton, butter, and cheese, after a reasonable price, not fully so good cheap as it was when the coin was at the perfectest, but within a fifth part of it or thereabouts.

10. I removed Farnham.

12. A proclamation set forth touching the coin: that whereas it was so that men for gain melted down the 9*d*. teston continually, and the 6*d*. also, there should be no person in any wise melt it down, upon pain to incur the penalty of the laws.

13. A letter directed to the Lord Treasurer, the Lord Great Master, and the Master of the Horse, to meet at London for the ordering of my coin and the payment of my debts; which done, to return and make report of their proceedings.

11. War proclaimed in Britain between the Emperor and the French by these terms: "Charles Roi d'Espagne et Duc de Milan," leaving out Emperor.

10. Four towns taken by the French soldiers that were the Emperor's in Piedmont, Chieri, and Amiens [St. Damian]. Also the Emperor's country there was spoiled, and 120 (130 *crossed out*) castles or fortresses taken. Proclamation made in Paris touching the bulls, that no man should go for them to Rome.
Other ships also taken by [the] Prior de Capua: merchants, to the number of a dozen. Prior [of] Capua had thirty-two galleys.

19. The French ambassador sent this news also, that the Turk had taken Tripoli.

20. The Secretary Cecil and Sir Philip Hoby sent to London to help the Lord Treasurer, etc., in the matters of the Bishops of Chichester, Worcester, and Durham, and examination of my sister's men.

18. Removing to Windsor.

20. The Lords at London, having tried all kinds of stamping, both of the fineness of nine, eight, six, four, and three, proved that without any loss but sufferable the coin might be brought to eleven (nine *crossed out*) ounces fine. For whereas it was thought before that the teston was through ill officers and ministers corrupted, it was tried that it had the valuation just, by eight sundry kinds of melting; and four hundred pounds of sterling money, a teston being but sixpence, made four hundred pounds 11 ounces fine of money sterling.

22. Whereupon they reported the same, and then it was concluded that the teston should be eleven ounces fine, the proportion of the pieces according to the gold, so that five shillings of silver should be worth five of gold.

23. Removing to Oatlands.

24. Agreed that the stamp of the shilling and sixpence should be: of [on] one side a king painted to the shoulders, in Parliament robes, and with a chain of the Order; five shillings, of silver, and half-five shillings, should be a king on horseback armed, with a naked sword hard to his breast. Also that York's mint, and Throckmorton's mint in the Tower, should go and work the fine standard. In the city of York and Canterbury should the small money be wrought of a baser state. Officers for the same were appointed.
A piece of Berwick wall fell because the foundation was shaken by working of a bulwark.

28. The Lord Marquis of Dorset, grieved much with the disorder of the Marches toward Scotland, surrendered the wardenship thereof to bestow where I would.

27. The wardenship of the North given to the Earl of Warwick. Removing to Hampton Court.

28. Commissioners appointed for sitting on the Bishop of Chichester and Worcester – three lawyers and three civilians.

10. The Imperial took the suburbs of Heding and burned them.

26. The passport of the Dowager of Scotland was made for a longer time, until Christmas, and also, if she were driven, to pass by land quietly into Scotland.

20. Mons. d'Angoulême was born, and the Duke of Vendôme had a son by the Princess of Navarre, his wife.

30. The feast of Michaelmas was kept by me in the robes of the Order.

OCTOBER

1. The commission for the making of five shillings, half-five shillings, groats, and sixpences 11 ounces fine, and pence with halfpennies and farthings four ounces fine, was followed and signed.

1. There was Rich, Lord Chancellor of England, did send back a letter for the execution of the commission for certain [ones] to sit on the Bishops of Chichester and Worcester because there were but eight hands [signed] to it.

2. I wrote a letter that I marvelled that he would refuse to sign that bill or deliver that letter that I had willed any one about me to write. Also that it should be a great impediment for me to send to all my Council and I should seem to be in bondage. But by oversight it chanced and [not] thinking the more the better.

5. Jarnac came in post for declaration of two things: the one that the Queen had a third son of which she was delivered, called le duc d'Angoulême, of which the King prayed me to be godfather. I answered

I was glad of the news and that I thanked him for that I should be godfather, which was a token of [the] good will he bore me. Also that I would dispatch for the accomplishment thereof the Lord Clinton, Lord Admiral of England.

He said he came also to tell me a second point of the good success of his master's wars. He told how the last month in Champagne beside Sedan, 1,000 horse Imperial with fivers Hungarians, Martin van Rossem being their captain and leader, entered the country and the alarum[?] came. The skirmish began so hot that the French horse, about two or three hundred men of arms, came out and took van Rossem's brother and slew divers. Also how in Piedmont, since the taking of the last four towns, three others were taken: Monteglio [Montechiaro], Saluzzo, and the town of Borgo. The Turks had come to Naples and spoiled the country and taken Ostia in the month of [the] Tiber. Also in Sicily he had taken a good haven and a town.

6. Jarnac departed, having been in the court under my lodging the night before. The Bishops of Worcester and Chichester were deposed for contempts.

7. There was appointed to go with the Lord Admiral, Mr. [Henry] Neville, Mr. Barnaby, gentleman of the chamber, Sir William Stafford, Sir Adrian Poynings, Sir John Norton, Sir John Tyrrell, knights, and Mr. Brooke.

8. Letters directed to the captains of the gendarmerie that they should muster the 8th of November, being the Sunday after All Hallows Day.

11. Harry, Marquis of Dorset, created Duke of Suffolk; John, Earl of Warwick, created Duke of Northumberland; William, Earl of Wiltshire, created Marquis of Winchester; Sir William Herbert created Earl of Pembroke and Lord of Cardiff. Mr. Sidney, Mr. Neville, Mr. Cheke, all three of the Privy Chamber, made knights. Also Mr. Cecil, one of the two chief Secretaries.

13. Proclamation signed touching the ceiling in of testons and groats, that they that list might come[?] to the mint and have fine silver of twelvepence for two testons.

3. Prior de Capua departed the French King's service and went to his order of knights in Malta, partly for displeasure to the Count Villiers, the Constable's brother-in-law, partly for that Malta was assailed often by the Turks.

7. Sir Thomas Palmer came to the Earl of Warwick, since that time Duke of Northumberland, to deliver him his chain, being a very fair one, for every link weighed one ounce, to be delivered to Jarnac and so to receive as much. Whereupon in my Lord's garden he declared a conspiracy. How at St. George's Day last, my Lord of Somerset (who the was going to the North if the Master of the Horse, Sir William Herbert, had not assured him on his honour that he should have no hurt) went to raise the people, and the Lord Grey before, to know who were his friends. Afterward a device was made to call the Earl of Warwick to a banquet with the Marquis of Northampton and divers other[s] and to cut off their heads. Also, if he found a bare company about them by the way, to set upon them.

11. He declared also that Mr. Vane had 2,000 men in readiness. Sir Thomas Arundel had assured my Lord that the Tower was safe. Mr. Partridge should raise London and take the Great Seal with the [ap]prentice[s] of London. Seymour and Hammond should wait upon him, and all the horse of the gendarmery should be slain.

15. Removing to Westminster, because it was thought this matter might easilier [*sic*] and surelier be dispatched there, and likewise all other [matters].

14. The Duke [of Somerset] sent for the Secretary Cecil to tell him he suspected some ill. Mr. Cecil answered that if he were not guilty he might be of good courage; if he were, he had nothing to say but to lament him. Whereupon the Duke sent him a letter of defiance and

called Palmer who, after denial [was] made of his declaration, was let go.

16. This morning none was at Westminster of the conspirators. The first was the Duke, who came, later than he was wont, of himself. After dinner he was apprehended. Sir Thomas Palmer [was taken] on the terrace walking there. Hammond, passing by Mr. Vice-Chamberlain's door, was called in by John Peers to make a match at shooting, and so [was] taken. Newdigate was called for as from my Lord his master and taken. Likewise were John Seymour and Davy Seymour. Arundel also was taken, as the Lord Grey, coming out of the country. Vane, upon two sendings of my Lord in the morning, fled at the first sending; he said my Lord was not stout, and if he could get home he cared for none of them all, he was so strong. But after[ward] he was found by John Peers in a stable of his man's at Lambeth, under the straw. These went with the Duke to the Tower this night, saving Palmer, Arundel, and Vane, who were kept in chambers here, apart.

17. The Duchess [of Somerset], Crane and his wife, with the chamber keeper, were sent to the Tower for devising these treasons; James Wingfield also, for casting out of bills seditious. Also Mr. Partridge was attached and Sir James [Thomas] Holcroft.

18. Mr. Bannister and Mr. Vaughan were attached and sent to the Tower, and so was Mr. Stanhope.

19. Sir Thomas Palmer confessed that the gendarmerie on the muster day should be assaulted by 2,000 footmen of Mr. Vane's, and my Lord's hundred horse, besides his friends which stood by, and the idle people which took his part. If he were overthrown he would (set upon *crossed out*) run through London and dry "Liberty, liberty," to raise the [ap]prentices, and if he could he would go to the Isle of Wight or to Poole.

22. The Dowager of Scotland was by tempest driven to land at Portsmouth, and so she sent word she would take the benefit of the safe-conduct to go by land and to see me.

26. She came from Portsmouth to Mr. White's house.

24. The Lords sat in the Star Chamber and there declared the matters and accusations laid against the Duke, meaning to stay the minds of the people.

25. Certain German princes in the beginning of this month desired aid in [the] cause of religion of 400,000 thalers, if they should be driven to make shift by necessity, and offered the like also if I entered into any war for them. Whereupon I called the Lords and considered, as appears by a scroll in the board at Westminster, and thereupon appointed that the Secretary Petre and Sir William Cecil [and] another Secretary [Wotton] should talk with the messenger to know the matter precisely and the names of those that would enter the confederacy.

28. The Dowager came to Sir Richard Cotton's house.

29. She came from Sir Richard Cotton's to the Earl of Arundel['s] to dinner and [was] brought to Mr. Browne's house, where met her gentlemen of Sussex.

30. She came and was conveyed by the same gentlemen to Guildford, where the Lord William Howard and the gentlemen of Surrey met her. All this month the Frenchmen continued spoiling of the Emperor's frontiers, and in a skirmish at Asti they slew (800 *crossed out*) 100 Spaniards.

31. A letter directed to Sir Arthur Darcy to take the charge of the Tower and to discharge Sir John Markham upon this: that, without making any of the Council privy, he suffered the Duke to walk abroad and certain letters to be sent and answered between Davy Seymour and Mrs.[?] Po[un]ings, with other divers suspicions.

17. There were letters sent to all emperors, kings, ambassadors, noblemen, men, and chief men in countries, of the late conspiracy.

31. She [the Dowager Queen of Scotland] came to Hampton Court, conveyed by the same Lord and gentlemen aforesaid, and two miles and a half from thence, in a valley, there met her the Lord Marquis of Northampton, accompanied with the Earl of Wiltshire, son and heir to the Lord High Treasurer Marquis of Winchester, the Lord Fitzwalter, son of the Earl of Sussex, the Lord Evre, the Lord Braye, the Lord Robert Dudley, the Lord Garret, Sir Nicholas Throckmorton, Sir Edward Rogers, and divers other gentlemen, besides all the gentlemen pensioners, men of arms, and ushers, sewers, and carvers, to the number of 120 gentlemen, and so she was brought to Hampton Court. At the gate thereof met her the Lady Marquis of Northampton, the Countess of Pembroke, and divers other ladies and gentlewomen to the number of threescore, and so she was brought to her lodging on the Queen's side, which was all hanged with arras, and so was the hall and all the other lodgings of mine in the house very finely dressed. And for this night and the next day all was spent in dancing and pastime, as though it were a court, and great presence of gentlemen resorted thither.

26. Letters were written forbecause of this business to defer the musters of the gendarmery till the [*blank*] day of December.

NOVEMBER

1. The Dowager perused the house of Hampton Court and saw some coursing of deer.

2. She came to the Bishop's Palace at London, and there she lay, and all her train lodged about her.

3. The Duke of Suffolk, the Earl of Warwick, [the Earl of] Wiltshire, and many other Lords and gentlemen were sent to her to welcome her and to say on my behalf that if she lacked anything she should have it, for her better furniture, and also [that] I would willingly see her the day

following.

The 26th of October Crane confessed the most part, even as Palmer did before, and more also; how that the place where the nobles should have been banqueted and their heads stricken off was the Lord Paget's house, and how the Earl of Arundel knew of the matter as well as he, by Stanhope who was a messenger between them. Also some part [of] how he went to London to get friends once in August last, feigning himself sick.

Hammond also confessed the watch he kept in his chamber at night. Brend also confessed much of this matter. The Lord Strange confessed how the Duke willed him to stir me to marry his third daughter, the Lady Jane, and willed him to be his spy in all matters of my doings and sayings and to know when some of my Council spoke secretly with me. This he confessed of himself.

4. The Duke of Suffolk [and] the Lord Fitzwalter, the Lord Braye, and divers other Lords and gentlemen, accompanied with his [Suffolk's] wife, the Lady Frances, the Lady Margaret, the Duchesses of Richmond and of Northumberland, the Lady Jane, daughter to the Duke of Suffolk, the Marchionesses of Northampton and Winchester, the Countesses of Arundel, Bedford, Huntingdon, and Rutland, with 100 other ladies and gentlewomen, went to her and brought her through London to Westminster. At the gate there received her the Duke of Northumberland, Great Master, and the Treasurer and Comptroller and the Earl of Pembroke with all the sewers and carvers and cupbearers, to the number of thirty. In the hall I met her with all the rest of the Lords of my Council, as the Lord Treasurer, the Marquis of Northampton, etc., and from the outer gate up to the presence chamber on both sides stood the guard. The court, the hall, and the stairs were full of servingmen; the presence chamber, great chamber, and her presence chamber, of gentlemen; and so, having brought her to her chamber, I retired to mine. I went to her to dinner. She dined under the same cloth of estate at my left hand. At her reward [rearward?] dined my cousin Frances and my cousin Margaret. At mine sat the French ambassador. We were served by two services: two sewers, cupbearers, carvers, and gentlemen. Her

maître d'hôtel came before her service, and mine officers before mine. There were two cupboards, one of gold four stages [in] height, another of massy silver six stages. In her great chamber dined at three boards the ladies only. After dinner, when she had heard some music, I brought her to the hall and so she went away.

5. The Duke of Northumberland, the Lord Treasurer, the Lord Marquis of Northampton, the Lord Privy Seal, and divers other[s] went to see her and to deliver a ring with a diamond and two nags, as a token from me.

6. The Duke of Northumberland with his band of [one] hundred, of which forty were in black velvet with white and black sleeves, sixty in cloth; the Earl of Pembroke with his band and fifty more; the Earl of Wiltshire with fifty-eight of his father's band; all the pensioners, men of warms, and the equerry, with divers ladies, [such] as my cousin Marg[ar]et, the Duchesses of Richmond and Northumberland, brought to the Queen to Shoreditch through Cheapside and Cornhill, and there met her gentlemen of Middlesex 100 horse, and so she was conveyed out of the realm, met in every shire with gentlemen.

8. The Earl of Arundel committed to the Tower with Sir [Thomas] Stradley [Stradling] and St. Albin his men, because Crane did more and more confess of him.

7. A Frenchman was sent again into France to be delivered again to the Frenchmen at the borders because of a murder he did at Dieppe, and thereupon he fled hither.

14. Answer was given to the Germans, which did require 400,000 thalers if need so required for maintenance of religion: first, that I was very well inclined to make peace, amity, or bargain with them I knew to be of mine religion (forbecause this messenger was sent only to know my inclination and will to enter, and not with full resolution of any matters). Secondly, I would know whether they could get unto them any such strength of other princes as were able to maintain the war and to do the reciproque to me again if need should so require. And therefore willed

those three princes – Duke Maurice of Saxony, the Duke of Mecklenburg, and the Marquis John of Brandenburg, from which he was sent – to open the matter to the Duke of Prussia and to all princes about them and somewhat to get the good will of Hamburg, Lübeck, Bremen, etc., showing them an inkling of the matter. Thirdly, I would have the matter of religion made more plain, lest when war should be made for other quarrels they should say it were religion. Fourthly, he should come with more ample commission from the same states to talk of the sum of money and other appurtenances. This answer was given lest, if I assented wholly at the first, they would declare mine intent to the Steads and whole senates and so to come abroad, whereby I should run into danger of breaking the league with the Emperor.

16. The Lord Admiral took his leave to go into France for [the] christening of the French King's son.

18. [Mr.] Fossey, secretary to the Duke Maurice, who was here for [the] matter above specified [*sentence unfinished*].

20. A proclamation appointed to go forth for that there went one before this time: that set prices of beef, oxen, and muttons, which was meant to continue but to November, whenas the Parliament should have been – to abrogate that and to appoint certain commissioners to cause the graziers to bring to the market and to sell at prices reasonable. And that certain overseers should be besides to certify of the justices' doings.

23. The Lord Treasurer [Winchester] appointed High Steward for the arraignment of the Duke of Somerset.
At this time Duke Maurice began to show himself friend to the Protestants, who before that time had appeared their enemy.

27. The [a]foresaid proclamation proclaimed.

17. The Earl of Warwick, Mr. Henry Sidney, Sir Harry Neville, and Sir Harry Gates did challenge all comers at tilt the 3rd of January and at tourney the 6th of January, and this challenge was proclaimed.

28. News came that Maximilian, coming out of Spain, nine of galleys with his stuff, and 120 jennets and his treasure was taken by the French.

24. The Lord Admiral entered France and came to Boulogne.

26. The captain of Portsmouth had word and commandment to bring the model of the castle and plate, to the intent it might be fortified, because Baron de la Garde had seen it, having an engineer with him and, as it was thought, had the plat of it.

30. Twenty-two peers, as nobles, besides the Council, heard Sir Thomas Palmer, Mr. Hammond, Mr. Crane, and Newdigate swear that their confessions were (was *in manuscript*) true, and they did say that that was said without any kind of compulsion, force, envy, or displeasure, but as favourably to the Duke as they could swear with safe conscience.

DECEMBER A D'NI 1551, 5 A R R E. 6. 5 CHARTA

1. The Duke of Somerset came to his trial at Westminster Hall. The Lord Treasurer sat as High Steward of England under the cloth of estate on a bench between two posts, three degrees (steps *crossed out*) high: all the Lords, to the number of twenty-six, *videlicet*:

DUKES
Suffolk
Northumberland

MARQUISES
Northampton

EARLS
Derby
Bedford
Huntingdon
Rutland
Bath
Sussex

Worcester
Pembroke

VISCOUNTS
Hereford

BARONS
Abergavenny
Audley
Wharton
Evre
Latimer
Burgh
Zouche
Stafford
Wentworth
Darcy
Stourton
Windsor
Cromwell
Cobham
Braye

These sat in a degree under and heard the matter debated. First, after the indictments [were] read, five in number[?], the learned counsel laid to my Lord of Somerset Palmer's confession. To which he answered that he never minded to raise the North and declared all ill he could devise of Palmer; but he was afraid for bruits, and that moved him to send to Sir William Herbert. Replied it was again, that the worse, Palmer was, the more he served his purpose. For the [planned] banquet: first he swore it was untrue and required more witnesses; when Crane's confession was read, he would have had him come face to face. For London: he meant nothing for hurt of any lord, but for his own defence. For the gendarmery: it were but a mad matter for him to enterprise, with his 100 against 900. For having men in his chamber at Greenwich, confessed by

74

Partridge: it seemed he meant no harm, because, when he could have done harm, he did it not. My Lord Strange's confession: he swore it was untrue, and the Lord Strange took his oath it was true. Newdigate's, Hammond's and Alexander Seymour's confessions he denied, because they were his men.

The lawyers rehearsed how to raise men at his horse for an ill intent, as to kill the Duke of Northumberland, was treason by an act 3 (2 *crossed out*) anno of my reign against unlawful assemblies: for to devise the death of the Lords was felony; to mind resisting his attachment was felony; to raise London was treason; and to assault the Lords was felony. He answered he did not intend to raise London, and that swore the witness[es] [who] were not there. His assembling of men was but for his own defence. He did not determine to kill the Duke of Northumberland, the Marquis, etc., but spoke of it and determined after[ward] the contrary; and yet seemed to confess he went about their death. The Lords went together. The Duke of Northumberland would not agree that any searching of his death should be treason. So the Lords acquitted him of high treason and condemned him of treason felonious, and so he was adjudged to be hanged. He gave thanks to the Lords for their open trial and cried mercy of the Duke of Northumberland, the Marquis of Northampton, and the Earl of Pembroke for his ill meaning against them, and made suit for his (life *added*), wife and children, servants and debts, and so departed without the ax of the Tower. The people, knowing not the matter, shouted half a dozen times so loud that from the hall (palace *crossed out*) door it was heard at Charing Cross plainly, and rumours went that he was quit of all.

2. The peace concluded by the Lord Marquis was ratified by me before the ambassador and delivered to him signed and sealed.

3. The Duke told certain Lords that were in the Tower that he had hired Berteville to kill them, which thing Berteville, examined on, confessed, and so did Hammond, that he knew of it.

7. I saw the musters of the new band [of] men of arms, 100 of my Lord Treasurer's, 100 of Northumberland, 100 Northampton, 50 Huntingdon, 50 Rutland, 120 of Pembroke, 50 Darcy, 50 Cobham, 100 Sir Thomas Cheyney, and 180 of the pensioners and their bands, with the old men of arms, all well-armed men, some with feathers, staves, and pencels of their colours, some with sleeves and half coats, some with bards and staves, etc. The horses all fair and great, the least would not have been given for less than £20. There was none under 14 handful and a half the most part, and almost all horses. With their guidon going before them, they passed twice about St. James's field and compassed it [a]round and so departed.

15. There were certain devices for laws delivered to my learned Council to pen, as by a schedule appeareth.

18. It was appointed I should have six chaplains ordinary, of which two [are] ever to be present and four always absent in preaching: one year two in Wales, two in Lancashire and Derby; next year two in the Marches of Scotland, two in Yorkshire; [the] 3rd year two in Devonshire, two in Hampshire; [the] 4th year two in Norfolk, Suffolk, and Essex, and two in Kent, Sussex, etc. These six to be Bill, Harley, (Estcourt *crossed out*), Perne, Grindal, (Bradford *crossed out*).

20. The Bishop of Durham was, for concealment of treason written to him and not disclosed at all till the party did open him, committed to the Tower.

21. Richard Lord Rich, Chancellor of England, considering his sickness, did deliver his seal to the Lord Treasurer, the Lord Great Master, and the Lord Chamberlain, sent to him for that purpose during the time of his sickness, and chiefly of the Parliament.

5. The Lord Admiral came to the French King and after[ward] was sent to the Queen and so conveyed to his chamber.

6. The Lord Admiral christened the French King's child and called him by the King's commandment Edward Alexander [Henry]. All that day there was music, dancing, and playing, with triumph in the court. But the Lord Admiral was sick of a double quartan. Yet he presented Barnaby to the French King, who took him to his chamber.

7. The treaty was delivered to the Lord Admiral; and the French King read it in open audience at mass, with the ratification of it. The Lord Admiral took his leave of the French King and returned to Paris very sick.
The same day the French King showed the Lord Admiral letters that came from Parma, how the Frenchmen had gotten two castles of the Imperials, and in the defence of the one of the Prince of Macedonia was slain on the walls and was buried with triumph at Parma.

22. The Great Seal of England [was] delivered to the Bishop of Ely to be keeper thereof during the Lord Rich's sickness.
The band of 100 men of arms, which my Lord of Somerset late had, appointed to the Duke of Suffolk.

23. Removing to Greenwich.

24. I began to keep holy this Christmas and continued till Twelfth Night.

26. Sir Anthony St. Ledger, for matters laid against him by the Bishop of Dublin, was banished [from] my chamber till he had made answer, and had the articles delivered him.

28. The Lord Admiral came to Greenwich.

30. Commission was made out to the Bishop of Ely, the Lord Privy Seal, Sir John Gates, Sir William Petre, Sir Robert Bowes, and Sir Walter Mildmay for calling in my debts.

JANUARY, 1552

1. Orders was taken with the chandlers of London for selling there tallow candles, which before some denied to do; and some were punished with imprisonment.

3. The challenge that was made in the last month was fulfilled. The challengers were:

The Earl of Warwick
Sir Harry Sidney
Sir Harry Neville
Sir Harry Gates

Defendants

The Lord William [Howard]
The Lord Fitzwalter
The Lord Ambrose [Dudley]
The Lord Robert [Dudley]
The Lord FitzWarren
Sir G[eorge] Howard
Sir Will. Stafford
Sir John Perrot
Mr. Norris
Mr. Digby
Mr. Warcopp
Mr. Courtney
Mr. Knollys
The Lord Braye
Mr. Paston
Mr. Carey
Sir Anthony Browne
Mr. Drury

These, eighteen in all, ran six courses apiece at tilt against the challengers, and (in the end *crossed out*) accomplished their courses right well, and so departed again.

5. There were sent to Guînes Sir Richard Cotton and Mr. Braye to take view of Calais, Guînes, and the marches, and with advice of the captains and engineers to devise some amendment, and thereupon to make me certificate, and upon mine answer to go further [in]to the matter.

4. It was appointed that if Mr. Stanhope lost Hull, then that I should no more be charged therewith, but that the town should take it and should have £40 a year for the repairing of the castle.

2. I received letters out of Ireland, which appear in the Secretary's hand. And thereupon the earldom of Thomond was by me given from O'Brien's heirs, whose father [Murrough O'Brien] was dead, and had it for term of life, to Donough, Baron of Ibrachan, and his heirs male. Also letters were written of thanks to the Earls of Desmond and Clanricard and to the Baron of Dungannon.

3. The Emperor's ambassador moved me severally that my sister Mary might have mass, which, with no little reasoning with him, was denied him.

6. The [a]foresaid challengers came in to the tourney, and the [a]foresaid defendants entered in after[ward] with two more with them – Mr. [William] Tyrrell and Mr. Robert Hopton – and fought right well, and so the challenge was accomplished. The same night was first a play; after a talk between one that was called Riches, and the other Youth, whether [one] of them was better. After some pretty reasoning there came in six champions of either side:

On Youth's side came:

My Lord Fitzwalter
My Lord Ambrose [Dudley]

Sir Anthony Browne
Sir William Cobham
Mr. Carey
Warcopp

On Riches' side:

My Lord FitzWarren
Sir Robert Stafford
Mr. Courtney
Digby
Hopton
Hungerford

All these fought two to two at barriers in the hall. Then came in two apparelled like Almains: the Earl of Ormonde and Jacques Granado; and two came in like friars; but the Almains would not suffer them to pass till they had fought. The friars were Mr. Drury and Thomas Cobham. After this followed two masques: one of men, another of women. Then a banquet of 120 dishes. This was the end of Christmas.

7. I went to Deptford to dine there and break up the hall.

8. Upon a certain contention between Lord Willoughby and Sir Andrew Dudley, captain of Guînes, for their jurisdiction, the Lord Willoughby was sent for to come over to the intent the controversy might cease and order might be taken.

12. There was a commission granted to the Earl of Bedford, and to the Mr. Vice-Chamberlain, and certain other[s], to call in my debts that were owing me, and the days past, and also to call in those that be past when the days be come.

17. There was a match run between six gentlemen of a side at tilt.

Of one side

The Earl of Warwick
The Lord Robert [Dudley]
Mr. Sidney
Mr. Neville
Mr. Gates
Anthony Digby
These won by 4 taints

Of the other side

The Lord Ambrose
The Lord Fitzwalter
Sir Francis Knollys
Sir Anthony Browne
Sir John Perrot
Mr. Courtney

18. The French ambassador moved that we should destroy the Scottish part of the Debatable Ground, as they had done ours. It was answered, first, the Lord Conyers, that made the agreement, made it none otherwise but as it should stand with his superior's pleasure. Whereupon, the same agreement being misliked because the Scottish part was much harder to overcome, word was sent to stay the matter; nevertheless the Lord Maxwell did upon malice to the English Debatables [i.e., Debatable Grounds] overrun them. Whereupon [it] was [now] concluded that, if the Scots will agree [to] it, the ground shall be divided; if not, then shall the Scots waste their Debatables, and we ours, commanding them by proclamation to depart.
This day the Steelyard put in their answer to a certain complaint that the Merchant Adventurers laid against them.

19. The Bishop of Ely, *custos sigilli*, was made Chancellor because as *custos sigilli* he could execute nothing in the Parliament that should be done but only to steal ordinary things.

21. Removing to Westminster.

22. The Duke of Somerset had his head cut off upon Tower Hill between eight and nine o'clock in the morning.

16. Sir William Pickering delivered a token to the Lady Elizabeth – a fair diamond.

18. The Duke of Northumberland, having under him 100 men of arms and 100 light horse, gave up the keeping of fifty men-at-arms to his son, the Earl of Warwick.

23. The sessions of Parliament began.

24. John Gresham was sent over into Flanders to show to the Fuggers, to whom I owe money, that I would defer it or, if I paid it, pay it in English to make them keep up their French crowns, with which I [was] minded to pay them.

25. The answer of the Steelyard was delivered to certain of my learned Council to look on and oversee.

27. Sir Ralph Vane was condemned of felony in treason, answering like a ruffian.
Paris arrived with horses and showed how the French King had sent me six curtails, two Turks, a Barbary [horse], two jennets, a stirring horse, and two little mules, and showed them to me.

29. Sir Thomas Arundel was likewise cast of felony in treason after long controversy; for the matter was brought in trial by seven of the clock in the morning [of the] 28th day; at noon the quest went together; they sat shut up together in a house, without meat or drink, because they could not agree, all that day and all night; this 29th day in the morning they did cast him.

FEBRUARY, A 6 REGNI EDWARDI 6

2. There was a King of Arms made for Ireland, whose name was Ulster, and his province was all Ireland, and he was the first [to be] fourth King

of Arms and the first Herald of Ireland.

The Emperor took the last month and this a million of pounds in Flanders.

6. It was appointed that Sir Philip Hoby should go to the Regent upon pretense of ordering of quarrels of merchants, bringing with him £63,000 in French crowns to be paid in Flanders at Antwerp to the Schetz and their family of debts I owe them, to the intent he might dispatch both under one.

8. Sir Miles Partridge was condemned of felony for the Duke of Somerset's matter, for he was one of the conspirators.

8. Fifty men-at-arms appointed to Mr. [Sir Ralph] Sadler.

9. John Beaumont, Master of the Rolls, was put in prison for forging a false deed from Charles Brandon, Duke of Suffolk, to the Lady Anne Powis of certain lands and leases.

10. Commission was granted out to thirty-two persons to examine, correct, and set forth the ecclesiastical laws. The persons' names were these:

The Bishops

Canterbury
Ely
London
Winchester
Exeter
Bath
Gloucester
Rochester

Civilians

Mr. Secretary Petre
Mr. Secretary Cecil
Mr. Traheron
Mr. Reed
Mr. Cook
May, Dean of [St.] Paul's
Skinner
[*Blank*]

The Divines

Taylor of Lincoln
Taylor of Hadleigh
Mr. Cox, almoner
Sir John Cheke
Sir Anthony Cooke
Petrus Martyr
Johannes à Lasco
Parker of Cambridge

Lawyers

Justice Bromley
Justice Hales
Gosnold
Goodrich
Stamford
Caryll
Lucas
Gawdy

10. Sir Philip Hoby departed with somewhat more crowns than came to 53,500 and odd pounds and had authority to borrow in my name of Lazarus Tucker £10,000 Flemish at 7 in the 100, for six months, to make

up the pay, and to employ that that was in bullion to bring over with him. Also, to carry 3,000 mark weight upon a license the Emperor granted the Schetz, which they did give me. After that to depart to Bruges, where the Regent lay, and there to declare to her the griefs [of] my subjects.

11. There was delivered of armour, by John [Thomas] Gresham, merchant, 1,100 pairs of corselets and horsemen harnesses, very fair.

14. It was appointed that the "Jesus of Lübeck," a ship of 800 tons, and the "Mary Gonston" of 600 tons, should be let out for one voyage to merchantmen for £1,000, they at the voyage to Levant end to answer the tackling [of] the ship, the ordnance, munition, and to leave it in that case they took it. Certain other of the worst of my ships were (was *in manuscript*) appointed to be sold.

9. Proclamation was made at Paris that the bands of the Dauphin, the Duke of Vendôme, the Count d'Enghien, the Constable of France, the Duke of Guise and of Aumale, the Count of Sancerre, the Maréchal St. André, Mons. de Jarnac's, and Tavannes', should, the 15th day of March, assemble at Troyes in Champagne to resist the Emperor. Also that the French King would go thither in person with 200 gentlemen of his household and 400 archers of his guard.

16. The French King sent his secretary, de l'Aubespine, to declare this voyage to him (Mr. Pickering *added*), and to desire him to take pains to go with him and to be a witness of his doings.

19. Whereupon it was appointed that he should have 2,000 crowns for his furnishment besides his diet, and Barnaby 800.

20. The Countess of Pembroke died.

18. The Merchant Adventurers put in their replication to the Steelyard's answer.

23. A decree was made by the board that, upon knowledge and information of their charters, they had found: first, that they were no sufficient corporation. Secondarily, their number, names, and nation was unknown. Thirdly, that when they had forfeited their liberties King Edward the Fourth did restore them on this condition: [that they] should colour no strangers' goods, which they had done. Also that, whereas in the beginning they shipped not past eight cloths, after[ward] 100, after[ward] 1,000, after that 6,000, now in their names were shipped 14,000 cloths in one year, and but 1,100 of all other strangers. For these considerations, sentence was given that they had forfeited their liberties and were in like case with other strangers.

28. There came ambassadors from Hamburg and Lübeck to speak on the behalf of the Steelyard merchants.

29. A Fleming would have searched the "Falcon" for Frenchmen. The "Falcon" turned, shot off, boarded the Fleming, and took him. Payment was made of £63,500 Flemish to the Fuggers, all saving £6,000, which he borrowed in French crowns, by Sir Philip Hoby.

MARCH

2. The Lord of Abergavenny was committed to ward for striking the Earl of Oxford in the chamber of presence.
The answer for the ambassadors of the Steelyard was committed to the Lord Chancellor, the two Secretaries, Sir Robert Bowes, Sir John Baker, Judge Montagu, Griffith Solicitor, Gosnold, Goodrich, and Brooke.

3. It was agreed that for better dispatch of things certain of the Council, with others joined with them, should overlook the penal laws and put certain of them in education. Other[s] should answer suitors; other[s] should oversee my revenues and the order of them, and also the superfluous, and the payments heretofore made; other[s] should have commission for taking away superfluous bulwarks.

1. Order was given, for defence of the merchants, to send four barks and two pinnaces to the sea.

4. The Earl of Westmorland, the Lord Wharton, the Lord Conyers, Sir Thomas Palmer, and Sir Thomas Chaloner were appointed in commission to meet with the Scottish ambassadors for the equal division of the ground that was called the Debatable.

6. The French ambassador declared to the Duke of Northumberland how the French King had sent him a letter of credit for his ambassador. After delivery [was] made of the letter, he declared how Duke Maurice of Saxony, the Duke of Mecklenburg, the Marquis of Brandenburg, the Count of Mansfeld, and divers other princes of Germany had made a league (sent embas *crossed out*) with his master, offensive and defensive: the French to go to Strassburg with 30,000 footmen and 8,000 horsemen, the Almains to meet with them there the 25th of this month, with 15,000 footmen and 5,000 horsemen. Also the city of Strassburg had promised them victuals; and [he] declared how the French King would send me ambassadors to have me into the same league. Also that the Marquis of Brandenburg and Count of Mansfeld had been privily conveyed to the French King's presence and were again departed to levy men, and he thought by this time they were in the field.

10. He declared the same thing to me in the same manner.

9. It was consulted touching the marts, and it was agreed that it was most necessary to have a mart in England for the enriching of the same, to make it the more famous, and to be less in other men's danger, and to make all things better cheap and more plentiful. The time was thought good to have it now, because of the wars between the French King and the Emperor. The places [which] were thought meetest: Hull for the east parts, Southampton for the south parts of England, as appeareth by two bills in my study. London also was thought no ill place; but it was appointed to begin with the other two.

11. The bills put up to the Parliament were overseen and certain of them were for this time thought meet to pass and to be read; other[s], for avoiding tediousness, to be omitted and no more bills to be taken.

15. Those that were appointed commissioners for the requests or for execution of penal laws or for overseeing of the courts received their commissions at my hand.

18. It was appointed that for the payment of £14,000 in the end of April there should be made an anticipation of the subsidy of London and of the Lords of my Council, which should go near to pay the same with good provision.

20. The French ambassador brought me a letter of credit from his master and thereupon delivered [to] me the articles of the league betwixt the Germans and him, desiring me to take part in (of *in manuscript*) the same league, which articles I have also in my study.

23. The merchants of England, having been long stayed, departed – in all about sixty sail, the wool fleet and all – to Antwerp. They were countermanded because of the mart, but it was too late.

24. Forasmuch as the exchange was stayed by the Emperor to Lyons, the merchants of Antwerp were sore afraid; and, [so] that the mart could not be without exchange, liberty was given to the merchants to exchange and rechange money for money.

A D'NI 1552, MENSE MARTIO, 6 CHARTA, REGNI REGIS E. 6 6 ANNO

26. Harry Dudley was sent to the sea with four ships and two barques for defence of the merchants, which were daily before robbed, who, as soon as he came to the sea, took two pirates' ships and brought them to Dover.

28. I did deny after a sort the request to enter into war, as appeareth by the copy of my answer in the study.

29. To the intent of the ambassador might more plainly understand my meaning, I sent Mr. Hoby and Mr. Mason to him to declare [to] him my intent more amply.

31. The Commissioners for the Debatable of the Scottish side did deny to meet, except a certain castle or pile might be first razed; whereupon letters were sent to stay our Commissioners from the meeting till they had further word.

10. Duke Maurice mustered at Arnstadt in Saxony all his own men – and left Duke August, the Duke of Anhalt, and the Count of Mansfeld – for the defence of his country, chiefly for fear of the Bohemians. The young[?] Landgrave Reiffenberg and other[s] mustered in Hesse.

14. The Marquis Albert of Brandenburg mustered his men two leagues from Erfurt and after[ward] entered the same, receiving of the citizens a gift of 20,000 florins, and he borrowed of them 60,000 florins, and so came to Schweinfurt, where Duke Maurice and all the German princes were assembled.

APRIL

2. I fell sick of the measles and the smallpox.

4. Duke Maurice with his army came to Augsburg, which town was at the first yielded to him and delivered into his hands; where he did change certain officers, restored their preachers, and made the town more free.

5. The Constable with the French army came to Metz, which was within two days yielded to him, where he found great provision of victuals, and that he determined to make the staple of victual for his journey.

8. He came to a fort wherein was an abbey called Gorze, and that fort abide[d] eighty cannon shot, at length came to a parley, where the Frenchmen got it, won it by assault, slew all save fifteen with the captain, whom he hung.

9. He took a fort called Marange and razed it.

12. The French King came to Nancy to go to the army and there found the Duchess and the young Duke of Lorraine.

13. The Maréchal St. André, with 200 men of arms and 2,000 footmen, carried away the young Duke, accompanied with few of his old men, toward France, to the Dauphin which lay at Reims, to the no little discontentation of his mother, the Duchess. He fortified also divers towns in Lorraine and put in French garrisons.

14. He departed from Nancy to the army, which lay at Metz.

7. Mons. Senarpont gave an overthrow to the captain of St. Omer, having with him 600 footmen and 200 horsemen.

15. The Parliament broke up, and because I was sick and not able to go well abroad as then, I signed a bill containing the names of the acts which I would have pass, which bill was read in the House.

16. Also I gave commission to the Lord Chancellor, two archbishops, two bishops, two dukes, two marquises, two earls, and two barons to dissolve wholly this Parliament.

18. The Earl of Pembroke surrendered his mastership of the horse, which I bestowed on the Earl of Warwick.

19. Also he [Pembroke] left fifty of his men of arms, of which twenty-five were given to Sir Philip Hoby and twenty-five to Sir John Gates.

21. It was agreed that commissions should go out for to take certificate of the superfluous church plate to my use and to see how it has been embezzled.
The French ambassador desired that, forasmuch as it was dangerous carrying for victuals from Boulogne to Ardres by land, that I would give license to carry by sea to Calais, and so from Calais to Andres on my ground.

22. The Lord Paget was degraded from the Order of the Garter for divers his offenses, and chiefly because he was no gentleman of blood, neither of father's side nor mother's side.
Sir Anthony St. Leger, who was accused by the Bishop of Dublin for divers brawling matters, was taken again into the Privy Chamber and sat amongst the Knights of the Order.

23. Answer was given to the French ambassador that I could not accomplish his desire, because it was against my league with the Emperor.

24. The Order of the Garter was wholly altered, as appears by the new statutes. There were elected Sir Andrew Dudley and the Earl of Westmoreland.

26. Mons. de Courrières came from the Regent [of the Netherlands] to desire that her fleet might safely upon occasion take harbour in my havens. Also he said he was come to give order for redressing all complaints of our merchants.

25. Whereas it was appointed that the £14,000 I owed in the last of April (February *crossed out*) should be paid, by the anticipation of the subsidy of London and of the Lords, because to exchange the same oversea[s] was [a] loss of the six[th] part of the money I did so send over, stay was made thereof and the payment appointed to be made out of £20,000 Flemish which I took up there, [at] 14 *per centum*, and so remained £6,000 thereof to be paid there the last of May.

30. Removing to Greenwich.

28. The charges of the mints were diminished £1,400, and there was left £600.

18. King Ferdinand, Maximilian his son, and [Albert] the Duke of Bavaria came to Linz to treat with Duke Maurice for a peace, where Maurice declared his griefs.

16. Duke Maurice's men received an overthrow at Ulm, where upon Marquis Albert [de]spoiled the country and gave them a day to answer.

31. A debt of £14,000 was paid to the Fuggers.

MAY

1. The Steelyard men received their answer, which was to confirm the former judgement of my Council

2. A letter was sent to the Fuggers from my Council to this effect: that I had paid £63,000 Flemish in February and £14,000 [Flemish] in April, which came to £87,000 [*sic*] Flemish, which was a fair sum of money to be paid in one year, (and the *crossed out*) chiefly in this busy world, whenas [money] is most necessary to be had for princes; besides this, that it was thought money should not now do him so much pleasure as at another time peradventure. Upon these considerations they had advised me to pay but £5,000 of the 45,000 I now owe and so to put over the rest according to the old interest, 14 *per cent.*, with which they desired him to take patience.

4. Mons. de Courrières received his answer, which was that I had long ago given order that the Flemish ships should not be molested in my havens, as it appeared because Frenchmen chasing Flemings into my havens could not get them because of the rescue they had. But I thought it not convenient to have more ships to come into my havens than I could well rule and govern. Also a note of divers complaints of my subjects was delivered to him.

10. Letters were sent to my ambassadors that they should move to the princes of Germany, to the Emperor, and to the French King, that if this treaty came to any effect or end I might be comprehended in the same. Commission was given to Sir John Gates, Sir Robert Bowes, the Chancellor of the [Count of] Augmentation[s], Sir Walter Mildmay, [and] Sir Richard Cotton to sell some part of the chantry lands and of the houses for the payment of my debts, which was £251,000 sterling at the

least.
Taylor, Dean of Lincoln, was made Bishop of Lincoln.
Hooper, Bishop of Gloucester, was made Bishop of Worcester and Gloucester.
Scory, Bishop of Rochester, was made Bishop of Chichester.
Sir Robert Bowes was appointed to be Master of the Rolls.

7. Commandment was given to the Treasurers that nothing of the subsidy should be disbursed but by warrant from [the] board, and likewise for Our Lady Day revenues.

14. The [Chief] Baron of the Exchequer, upon the surrender made by Justice Lyster, [was] made chief justice; the attorney, chief baron; the solicitor general, attorney; and the solicitor of the Augmentation[s] Gosnold, general solicitor; and no more solicitors to be in the Augmentation[s] Court. Also there were appointed eight sergeants of the law against Michaelmas next coming: Gawdy, Stamford, Caryll [*the remaining names are omitted*].

16. The muster was made of all the men-at-arms, saving fifty of Mr. Sadler's, twenty-five of Mr. Vice-Chamberlain, and twenty-five [of] Sir Philip Hoby, and also of all the pensioners.

17. The progress was appointed to be by Portchester [Portsmouth] to Poole in Dorsetshire and so through Salisbury homeward to Windsor.

18. It was appointed that money should be cried down in Ireland after a pay which was of money at midsummer next; in the mean season the thing to be kept secret and close. Also that Pirry, the mint master, (should overtake *crossed out*) taking with him Mr. Brabazon, Chief Treasurer of the realm, should go to the mines and see what profit may be taken of the ore that the Almains had dug in a mine of silver; and if it would quit cost or more, to go forward withal; if not, to leave off and discharge all the Almains.
Also that 500 of the 2,000 soldiers there being should be cut off, and as many more as would go to serve the French King or the Emperor,

leaving sufficient at home. No fortifications to be made also yet for a time in no place unfortified; and many other articles were concluded for Ireland.

20. Sir Richard Wingfield, [John] Rogers, and [Sir Andrew Dudley] were appointed to view the state of Portsmouth, and to bring again their opinions touching the fortifying thereof.

4. The French King, having passed the straits of Lorraine, came to Saverne, four miles from Strassburg and was victualed by the country but denied of passage through their own.

3 PAGINA CHARTAE 6

21. Answer came from the Fuggers that for the deferring of £30,000, parcel of [£]45,000, he was content, and likewise for August pay, [just] so he might have paid him £20,000 as soon as might be.

22. It was appointed that, forasmuch as there was much disorder on the Marches on [the] Scotland side, both in vain fortifications of some places and negligent looking to other forts, the Duke of Northumberland, General Warden thereof, should go down and view it and take order for it and return home with speed. Also a pay of £10,000 to go before him.

23. It was appointed that these bands of men of arms should go with me [on] this progress:

Lord Treasurer	30
Lord Great Master	25
Lord Privy Seal	30
Duke of Suffolk	25
Earl of Warwick	25
Earl of Rutland	15
Earl of Huntingdon	25
Earl of Pembroke	50
Lord Admiral	15

Lord Darcy	30
Lord Cobham	20
Lord Warden	20
Mr. Vice-Chamberlain	15
Mr. Sadler	10
Mr. Sidney	10

26. It was appointed that Thomas Gresham should have paid him out of the money that came of my debts £7,000, for to pay £6,800 the last of the month, which he received the same night.

28. The same Thomas Gresham had £9,000 paid him toward the payment of £26,000 which the Fuggers required to be paid at the Paschal Mart [Easter Fair]. For he had taken by exchange from hence £5,000 and odd, and £10,000 he borrowed of the Schetz, and ten [thousand] of Lazarus Tucker. So there was in the whole [£]25,[000], of which was paid the last of April 14,[000] so the[re] remain £11,000 and £9,000, which I now made over by exchange, which made £20,000 to pay the Fuggers with.

30. I received advertisement from Mr. Pickering that the French King went from Saverne to Arromaches [Augersmache?], which was yielded to him, [from] thence to Limbourg and so toward Spires, his army to be about 20,000 footmen and 8,000 horsemen well-appointed, besides rascals. He had with him fifty pieces of artillery, of which [there] were twenty-six cannons and six organs and [a] great number of boats. From Limbourg – partly doubting Duke Maurice's meaning, partly for lack of victuals, and also because he had word that the Regent's army, of which were guides the Count of Egmont, Mons. de Rie, Martin van Rossem, and Duke [Adolf] of Holest [Holstein?], to the number of 16,000 footmen and 6,000 horsemen, had invaded Champagne and fortified Aschenay [Stenay] – he retired homeward till he came to Striolph [Struthof?] and there commanded all unprofitable carriage[s] and men should depart to Chalons, and [he] sent to the Admiral to come to him with 6,000 Swiss, 4,000 Frenchmen, 1,500 horsemen, and thirty pieces

of ordnance, meaning as it was thought to do some enterprise about Luxemburg, or to recover Aschenay [Stenay], which the Regent had fortified. There died in this journey 2,000 men for lack of good victuals. For eight days they had but bread and water, and they had marched sixty Dutch miles at the least and passed many a strait very painfully and laboursomely.

19. Duke Maurice, coming from Augsburg in great haste, came this day to the first passage, called the Clouse, which the Emperor had caused to be strongly fortified and victualed, a passage through a hill, cut out artificially on the way to Innsbruck, and there was a strong bulwark made hard by it which he won, after a long fight, within (no less than *crossed out*) an hour and a half by assault and took and slew all that were within; and that night he marched through that hill into a plain where he looked for to see twelve ensigns of landsknechts of his enemies. But they retired to the second strait, and yet divers of them were both slain and taken; and so that night he lodged in the plain at the entry of the second passage where [there] were five forts and one castle, which with ordnance slew some of Duke Maurice's men.

20. This morning the Duke of Mecklenburg, with three thousand footmen, cast a bridge over a river five miles beneath [a] sluice and came and gave assault behind the sluice, and Duke Maurice gave assault in the face, and the countrymen of Tyrol, for hate of the Spaniards, help[ed] Duke Maurice, so that the five forts were won by assault and the castle yielded upon condition to depart, not to serve in three months after[ward] the Emperor. In this enterprise he slew and took 3,500 persons and twenty-three pieces of artillery and 240,000 s[cutes]. The Emperor, hearing of this, departed by night from Innsbruck forty miles that night in post; he killed two of his jennets and rode continually every night; first to Brixenium and after[ward], for doubt of the Cardinal of Ferrara's army, turned to Villach in Carinthia the thirtieth of May, tarrying[?] for the Duke of Alva, who should come to him with 2,000 Spaniards and 3,000 Italians that came from Parma. Also the Emperor

delivered Duke Frederick from captivity, and sent him through Bohemia into Saxon to raise a power against Duke Maurice, his nephew.

22. Duke Maurice, after that Hall (Hala *in manuscript*) and divers other towns about Innsbruck in Tyrol had yielded, came to Innsbruck and there caused all the stuff to be brought to the market place and took all that pertained to Imperialists as confiscate; the rest he suffered the townsmen to enjoy. He took there fifty pieces of ordnance, which he conveyed to Augsburg, for that town he fortified and made it his staple of provision.

7 CHARTA, A D'NI 1552 MENSE JUNIO
June

2. Sir John Williams, who was committed to the Fleet for disobeying a commandment given to him for not paying any pensions without making my Council privy, upon his submission was delivered out of prison.

4. Beaumont, M[aste]r of the Rolls, did confess his offenses, who [how] in his office of wards he had brought land with my money, had lent it, and kept it from me to the [value of] £9,000 and above, more than this twelvemonth, and £11,000 in obligations; who [how], he being judge in the Chancery, between the Duke of Suffolk and the Lady Powis, took her title and went about to get it into his hands, paying a sum [of] money and letting her have a farm of a manor of his and caused an indenture to be made falsely with the old Duke's counterfeit hand to it, by which he gave these lands to the Lady Powis and went about to make twelve men perjured. Also how he had concealed the felony of his man, to the sum of £200 which he stole from him, taking the money to his own hand again. For these considerations he surrendered into my hands all his offices, lands, and goods moveable and unmovable, toward the payment of this debt and of the fines due to these particular faults by him done.

6. The Lord Paget, Chancellor of the Duchy [of Lancaster], confessed how he, without commission, did sell away my lands and great timber woods; how he had taken great fines of my lands to his said peculiar

profit and advantage, never turning any to my use or commodity; how he made leases in reversion for more than twenty-one years. For these crimes and other like recited before, he surrendered his office and submitted himself to those fines that I or my Council would appoint, to be levied of his goods and lands.

7. Whalley, Receiver of Yorkshire, confessed how he lent my money upon gain and lucre; how he paid one year's revenue over with the arrearages of the last; how he bought my own land with my money; how in his accounts he had made many false suggestions; how at the time of the fall of money he borrowed divers sums of money and had allowance for it after[ward], by which he gained £500 at one crying down, the whole sum being £2,000 and above. For these and suchlike considerations he surrendered his office and submitted to fines which I or my Council should assign him, to be levied of his goods and lands.

8. The Lords of the Council sat at [the] Guildhall in London, where in the presence of a thousand people they declared to the Mayor and brethren their slothfulness in suffering unreasonable prices of things, and to craftsmen their wilfulness, etc., telling them that if upon this admonition they did not amend, I was wholly determined to call in their liberties as confiscate and to appoint officers that should look to them.

10. It was appointed that the Lord Grey of Wilton should be pardoned of his offenses and delivered out of the Tower.
Whereas Sir Philip Hoby should have gone to Calais with Sir Richard Cotton and William Barnes, auditor, it was appointed [that] Sir Anthony. St. Leger, Sit Richard Cotton, and Thomas Mildmay should go thither, carrying with them £10,000 to be received out of the Exchequer.
Whereas it was agreed that there should be a pay now made to Ireland of £5,000, and then the money to be cried down, it was appointed that 3,000 weight which I had in the Tower should be carried thither and coined at 3 *denar.* fine, and that incontinent the coin should be cried down.
Also… of… tenes play should be shifted [?] to the porter's lodge.[16]

12. Because Pirry tarried here for the bullion, William Williams, assay master, was put in his place to view the mines with Mr. Brabazon or him who[m] the Deputy should appoint.

13. Bannister and Crane – the one for his large confession, the other because little matter appeared against him – were delivered out of the Tower.

16. The Lord Paget was brought into the Star Chamber and there declared effectuously his submission by word of mouth and delivered it in writing. Beaumont, who had before made his confession inwriting, began to deny it again, but after being called before my Council, he did confess it again and there acknowledged a fine of his land and signed an obligation in surrender of all his goods.

17. Mons. de Courrières took his leave.

2. The French King won the castle of Rodemanche.

3. Certain horsemen of the Regent's came and set upon the French King's baggage and slew divers of the carters, but at length with some loss of the Frenchmen they were compelled to retire. The French King won Mount Saint Jean.

4. The French King came to Damvillers, which was a strong town, and besieged it, making three breaches.

12. The town was yielded to him, with the captain. He found in it 2,500 footmen, 200 horsemen, 63 brass great-pieces, 300 harquebuses a croc, much victuals, and much munitions, as he did write to his ambassador.

19. It was appointed that the Bishop of Durham's matter should stay till the end of the progress.

---

[16] The entire entry was crossed out, making it almost illegible.

20. Beaumont in the Star Chamber confessed, after a little sticking upon the matter, his faults, to which he had put to his hand.

23. It was agreed that the bands of men of arms appointed to Mr. Sidney, Mr. Vice-Chamberlain, Mr. Hoby, and Mr. Sadler should not be furnished but left off.

25. It was agreed that none of my Council should move me in any suit of land – for forfeits above £20, for reversions of leases, or any other extraordinary suits – till the state of my revenues were further known.

15. The French King came to a town standing on the river of Meuse called Yvoix, which gave him many hot skirmishes.

18. The French King began his battery to the walls.

14. The townsmen of Montmédy gave a hot skirmish to the French and slew Mons. de Toge's brother and many other gentlemen of the camp.

12. The Prince of Salerno, who had been with the French King to treat with him touching the matters of Naples, was dispatched in post with this answer: that the French King would aid him with 13,000 footmen and 1,500 horsemen, in the French wages, to recover and conquer the kingdom of Naples, and [that] he should marry, as some said, the French King's sister Madam Marguerite. The cause why this Prince rebelled against the Emperor was partly the uncourteous handling of the Viceroy of Naples, partly ambition.

18. The Flemings made an invasion into Champagne, insomuch that the Dauphin had almost been taken, and the Queen, lying at Chalons, sent some of her stuff toward Paris.

12. Also another company took the town of Guise and [de]spoiled the country also.

22. Mons. de Taille [Thais] was [sent] for to raise the arrear bands and legionnaires of Picardy and Champagne, to recover Guise and invade Flanders.

27. Removing to Hampton Court.

30. It was appointed that the Steads should have this answer: that those cloths which they had bought to carry over, to the summer of 2,000 cloths and off, should be carried at their old custom, [just] so they were carried within six weeks; and likewise all commodities they brought in till Our Lady Day [March 25] in Lent next; in all other points the old decree to stand, till by a further communication the matter should be ended and concluded.
The Lord Paget was licensed to tarry at London and thereabout till Michaelmas, because he had no provision in his country.

26. Certain of the heralds – Lancaster and Portcullis – were committed to ward for counterfeiting Clarenceux seal to get money by giving of arms.

23. The French King, having received divers skirmishes of the townsmen, and chiefly two – the one when they slew the French light horse lying in a village by the town, the other when they entered into the camp and pulled down tents, which two skirmishes were given by the Count of Mansfeld, governor of the town and [of] the Duchy of Luxemburg, and his three hundred light horse – [and] understanding by the treason of four priests the weakest part of the town, so affrayed the townsmen and the Flemish soldiers that they by threatenings compelled their captain, the Count, that he yielded himself and the gentlemen prisoners, [and] the common soldiers [were permitted] to depart with white wands in their hands. This town was well fortified, victualed, and furnished.

24. The town of Montmédy yielded to the French King, which before had given him a hot skirmish.

JULY

4. Sir John Gates, Vice-Chamberlain, was made Chancellor of the Duchy of [Lancaster].

7. Removing to Oatlands.

5. The Emperor's ambassador delivered the Regent's letter, being of this effect: that, whereas I was bound by a treaty with the Emperor made a D'ni 1542 at Utrecht, that if any many did invade the Low Count[r]ies I should help him with 5,000 footmen or 700 crowns a day during four months and make war with him within a month after the request [was] made, and now the French King had invaded Luxemburg – desiring me to follow the effect of the treaty.

7. The names of the commissioners were added and made more, both in the debts, the surveying of the courts, the penal laws, etc., and that became my Lord Chamberlain, my Lord Privy Seal, Mr. Vice-Chamberlain, and Mr. Secretary Petre went with me [on] this progress.

8. It was appointed that 50 *li.* weight of gold (bullion *crossed out*) should be coined after the new standard, to carry about this progress, which makes £1,500 sterling.

9. The Chancellor of the Augmentations was willed to surcease his commission, given him [in] the third year of our reign.

3. Mons. de Bossu, grand Esquire to the Emperor, was made general of the army in the Low Countries, and Mons. de Praet over the horsemen.

10. it was appointed here that, if the Emperor's ambassador did move any more for help or aid, this answer should be sent him by two of my Council: that [in] this progress-time my Council was dispersed; I would work by their advice and he must tarry till the matter were concluded and their opinions heard. Also I had committed the treaty to be considered by divers learned men, etc. And if another time he would press me, then answer to be made that I trusted the Emperor would not

wish me in these young years, having felt them so long, to enter into them; how I had amity sworn with the French King, which I could not break; and therefore, if the Emperor thought it so meet, I would be a mean for a peace between them, but not otherwise. And if he did press the treaty, lastly to conclude that the treaty did not bind me which my father had made, being against the profit of my realm and country; and to desire a new treaty to be made between me and the Emperor, which (being pressed to the Emperor in the last wars) he answered that he marveled what we meant, for we are bound (quoth[?] the Emperor) and not you. Also the Emperor had refused to fulfil it divers times, both in not letting pass horses, armour, munition, etc., which were provided by me for the wars, as also in not sending aid upon the foraging of the low country of Calais.

12. Letter was written to Sir Peter Meutas, Captain of the Isle of Guernsey, both to command him that divine service may there be used as in England, and also that he take heed to the church plate that it be not stolen away but kept safe till further order be taken.

9. The French King came to the town of Avesnes in Hainault, where, after he had viewed the town, he left it and besieged a pile called Tirloc; but the bailiff of the town, perceiving his departure, gave the onset of his rearward with 2,000 footmen and 500 horsemen, and slew 500 Frenchmen. After this and the winning of certain holds of little force, the French King returned into France and divided his army into divers good towns to rest them, because divers were sick of the flux and such other diseases – meaning shortly to increase his power and so to go forward with his enterprise.

12. Frederick, Duke of Saxony, was released from his imprisonment and sent by the Emperor into his own country, to the great rejoicing of all the Protestants.

5. The Emperor declared that he would [accept] none of those articles to which Duke Maurice agreed, and the King of [the] Romans also. The copy of them remains with the Secretary Cecil.

Marquis Albert of Brandenburg did great harm in the country of Franconia, burned all towns and villages about Nürnberg and compelled them to pay to the princes of his league 200,000 thalers, ten of the fairest pieces of ordnance, and 150 quintals of powder. After that he went to Frankfurt to distress certain soldiers gathered there for the Emperor.

15. Removing to Guildford.

21. Removing to Petworth.

23. The answer was made to the Emperor's ambassador, touching the aid he required, by Mr. Wotton and Mr. Hoby, according to the first article *supra*.

24. Because the number of bands that went with me [on] this progress made the train great, it was thought good they should be sent home, save only 150 which were picked out of all the bands. This was because the train was thought to be near 4,000 horse, which were enough to eat up the country; for there was little meadow nor hay all the way as I went.

25. Removing to Cowdray, Sir Anthony Browne's house.

27. Removing to Halnaker.

30. Whereas it had been before devised – that the new fort of Berwick should be made with four bulwarks, and for making of two of them the wall of the town should be left open on the enemy's side a great way together, which thing had been both dangerous and chargeable – it was agreed the wall should stand, and two slaughterhouses to be made upon to scour the outer curtains, a great rampart to be made within the wall, a great ditch within that, another wall within that with two other slaughterhouses, and a rampart within that again.

26. The Flemings entered in great numbers into the country of Thérouanne, whereupon 500 men of arms arose of Frenchmen and gave the onset on the Flemings, overthrew them and slew of them 1,435, whereof were 150 horsemen.

31. It was appointed upon my Lord of Northumberland's request that he should give half his fee to the Lord Wharton and make him his deputy warden there.

AUGUST

2. Removing to Warblington.

2. The Duke of Guise was sent into Lorraine to be the French King's lieutenant there.

4. Removing to Waltham.

8. Removing to Portsmouth.

9. In the morning I went to Chaderton's bulwark, and viewed also the town. At afternoon went to see the storehouse, and there took a boat and went to the wooden tower and so to Hasleford. Upon viewing of which things there were devised two forts to be made upon the entry of the haven, one where Ridley's tower stands, upon the neck that makes the Camber, the other upon a little neck standing on the other side [of] the haven, where stood an old bulwark of wood. This was devised for the strength of the haven. It was meant that that to town side should be both stronger and larger.

10. Harry Dudley, who lay at Portsmouth with a warlike company of 140 good soldiers, was sent to Guînes with his men because the Frenchmen assembled in those frontiers in great numbers. Eod[ie]. Removing to Titchfield, the Earl of Southampton's house.

14. Removing to Southampton.

16. The French ambassador came to declare how the French King meant to send one that was his lieutenant in the civil law at Paris to declare which of our merchants' matters have [been] adjudged on their side, and which against them, and for what consideration.

16. Removing to Beaulieu.
The French ambassador brought news how the city of Siena had been taken by the French side on St. James's Day by one that was called the Count Perigliano and other Italian soldiers, by treason of some within the town, and all the garrison of the town, being Spaniards, were either taken or slain. Also how the Marshal Brissac had recovered Saluzzo and taken Verucca. Also how Villebon had taken Turnhout and Montreuil in the Low Country.

18. Removing to Christchurch.

21. Removing to Woodlands.
In this month, after long business, Duke Maurice and the Emperor agreed on a peace. But Marquis Albert of Brandenburg would not consent thereto, but went away with his army to Spires, and Worms, Cologne, and Trèves, taking large sums of money of all cities which he passed, but chiefly of the clergy. Duke Maurice's soldiers, perceiving Marquis Albert would enter into no peace, went almost all to the Marquis' services, among which were principal[ly] the Count of Mansfeld, Baron Heideck, and a colonel of 3,000 footmen and 1,000 horsemen called Reiffenberg. So that, of 7,000 which should be sent into Hungary against the Turks, there remained not 3,000. Also the Duke of Württemberg did secretly let go 2,500 of the best soldiers in Germany to the service of Marquis Albert. So that his power was now very great. Also in this month the Emperor departing from Villach came to Innsbruck, and so to Munich and to Augsburg, accompanied with 8,000 Spaniards and Italians and a little band of a few ragged Almains. Also in this mouth (about the middle thereof *crossed out*) did the Turks win the city of Temesvár in Transylvania and give a battle to the Christians, in which was slain Count Pallavicino and 7,000 Italians and Spaniards. Also in this month did the Turks' navy take the Cardinal of Trent's two brothers, and seven galleys, and had in chase thirty-nine other[s]. Also in this month did the Turks' navy land at Terracina in the kingdom of Naples, and the Prince of Salerno set forward with 4,000 Gascons and 6,000 Italians, and the Count Perigliano [Pitigliano] brought to his aid

5,000 men of those that were at the enterprise of Siena. Also the Marshal Brissac won a town in Piedmont called Bussac[?].

24. Removing to Salisbury.

26. Upon my Lord of Northumberland's return out of the North, it was appointed for the better strengthening of the Marches that no one man should have two offices, and there[fore] Mr. Strelley, Captain of Berwick, should leave the wardenship of the East Marches to the Lord Evre. And upon the Lord Conyers' resignation, the captainship of the castle of Carlisle was appointed to Sir [Ralph] Gray, and the wardenship of the West Marches to Sir Richard Musgrave.

27. Sir Richard Cotton made Comptroller of the Household.

28. Removing to Wilton.

30. Sir Anthony Aucher was [ap]pointed to be Marshal of Calais, and Sir Edward Grimston Comptroller of Calais.

22. The Emperor, being at Augsburg, did banish two preachers (Protestants) out of Augsburg under pretense that they preached seditiously, and left Mecardus the chief preacher and six other Protestant preachers in the town, giving the magistrates leave to choose other[s] in their place that were banished.

29. The Emperor caused eight Protestant citizens of the town to be banished, of them that went to the fair at Linz, under pretense that they, taking Marquis Albert's part, would not abide his presence.

SEPTEMBER

2. Removing to Mottisfont, my Lord Sandys' house.

5. Removing to Winchester.

7. From thence to Basing, my Lord Treasurer's house.

10. And so to Donnington Castle, beside the town of Newbury.

12. And so to Reading.

15. And so to Windsor.

8 CHARTA, MED SEPTEMBRIS, A D'NI 1552, A REGNI R E. 6 6

16. Stuckley, being lately arrived out of France, declared how that the French King – being wholly persuaded that he [Stuckley] would never return again into England because he came away without leave upon the apprehension of the Duke of Somerset, his old master – declared to him his intent that, upon a peace made with the Emperor, he meant to besiege Calais and thought surely to win it by the way of Sandhills, for having Risebank, both to famish the town and also to beat the market place; and [he] asked Stuckley's opinion. When Stuckley had answered he thought it impossible, then he told him that he meant to land in England in an angle thereof about Falmouth, and said the bulwarks might easily be won, and [that] the people were papistical; also that Mons. de Guise at the same time should enter into England by Scotland side, with the aid of the Scots.

19. After long reasoning it was determined, and a letter was sent in all haste to Mr. Morison, willing him to declare to the Emperor that I, having pity, as all other Christian princes should have, on the invasion of Christendom by the Turk, would willingly join with the Emperor and other states of the empire, if the Emperor could bring it to pass in some league against the Turk and his confederates, but not to be acknown of the French King; only to say that he hath no more commission, but if the Emperor would send a man into England, he should know more. This was done on intent to get some friends. The reasonings be in my desk.

21. A letter was sent, only to try Stuckley's truth, to Mr. Pickerling, to know whether Stuckley did declare any piece of this matter to him. Barnaby was sent home.

23. The Lord Grey was chosen Deputy of Calais in the Lord Willoughby's place, who was thought unmeet for it.

24. Sir Nicholas (Thomas *crossed out*) Wentworth was discharged of the portership of Calais, and one Cotton was put into it. In consideration of his age, the said Sir Nicholas Wentworth had a hundred pound pension.

26. Letters were sent for the discharge of the men of arms at Michaelmas next following.

27. The young lords' table was taken away, and the masters' of request, and the serjeant of arms', and divers other extraordinary allowances.

26. The Duke of Northumberland, the Marquis of Northampton, the Lord Chamberlain, Mr. Secretary Petre, and Mr. Secretary Cecil ended a matter at Eton College between the master and the fellows and also took order for the amendment of certain superstitious statutes.

28. Removing to Hampton Court.

29. Two lawyers came from the French King to declare what things had passed with the Englishmen in the King's Privy Council, what and why against them, and what was now in doing and with what diligence. Which when they had eloquently declared, they were referred to London, where there should speak with them Mr. Secretary Petre, Mr. Wotton, and Mr. Thomas Smith. Where by them was declared the griefs of our merchants, which came to the sum of fifty thousand pounds, and upwards; to which they gave little answer but that they would make report when they came home because they had yet no commission, but only to declare [to] us (use *in manuscript*) the causes of things done. The first day of this month the Emperor departed from Augsburg toward Ulm, and thanking the citizens for their steadfast sticking to him in these parlous times, he passed by them to Strassburg, accompanied only with 4,000 Spaniards, 5,000 Italians, 12,000 Almains, and 2,000 horsemen, and thanking also them of Strassburg for their goodwill they bore him, that they would not let the French King come into their town, he went to

Wissembourg and so to Spires and came thither the 23rd of this month. Of which thing the French King [when] advertised summoned an army to Metz and went thitherward himself, sent a pay of three months to [the] Marquis Albert and the Rhinegrave and his band, also willing him to stop the Emperor's passage into these Low Countries and to fight with him.

27. The matter of the Debatable [Ground] was agreed upon according to the last instructions.

6. Duke Maurice, with 4,000 footmen and 1,000 horsemen, arrived at Vienna, against the Turks.

21. Marquis Hans of Brandenburg came with an army of 13,000 footmen and 1,500 horsemen to the Emperor's army, and many Almain soldiers increased his army wonderfully. For he refused none.

OCTOBER

3. Because I had a pay of £48,000 to be paid in December and had as yet but £14,000 beyond sea to pay it withal, the merchants did give me a loan of £40,000, to be paid by them the last of December and to be repaid again by me the last of March. The manner of levying this loan was of[f] the cloths after the rate of 20s. of[f] a cloth. For they carried out at this shipping 40,000 broadcloths. This grant was confirmed the 4th day of this month by a company assembled of 300 Merchant Adventurers.

2. The bulwarks of earth and boards in Essex, which had a continual allowance of soldiers in them, were discharged, by which was saved presently £500, and hereafter £700 or more.

4. The Duke [of] Alva and the Marquis of Marignano set forth with a great part of the Emperor's army, having all the Italians and Spaniards with them, toward Trèves, where the Marquis Albert had set ten ensigns

of lance knights to defend it, and tarried himself with the rest of his army at Landan beside Spires.

6. Because Sir Andrew Dudley, Captain of Guînes, had indebted himself very much by his service at Guînes, also because it should seem injurious to the Lord Willoughby that for the contention between him and Sir Andrew Dudley he should be put out of his office, therefore it was agreed that the Lord William Hard should be Deputy of Calais and the Lord Grey Captain of Guînes.
Also it was determined that Sir Nicholas Strelley should be captain of the new fort at Berwick, that Alexander Brett should be porter, and one Rokesby should be marshal.

7. Upon report of letters written from Mr. Pickering – how that Stuckley had not declared to him, all the while of his being in France, no one word touching the communication afore specified and declared, and also how Mr. Pickering thought and certainly advertised that Stuckley never heard the French King speak no such word, nor never was in credit with him or the Constable, save once when he became an interpreter between the Constable and certain English pioneers – he was committed to the Tower of London. Also the French ambassador was advertised how we had committed him to prison for that he was untruly slandered the King our (my *crossed out*) good brother (as other such renegades do daily the same). This was told him to make him suspect the English renegades that be there. A like letter was sent again to Mr. Pickering.

8. The Seigneur de Villandry came in post from the French King with this message: First, that although Mr. Sidney's and Mr. Winter's matters were justly condemned, yet the French King (because they both were my servants, and one of them about me) was content *gratuito* to give Mr. Sidney his ship and all the goods in her, and Mr. Winter his ship and all his own goods. Which offer was refused, saying we required nothing *gratuito*, but only justice and expedition. Also Villandry declared that the King his master wished that an agreement were made between the ordinances and customs of England and France in marine affairs; to

which was answered that our ordinances were nothing but the civil law, and certain very old additions of the realm; that we thought it reason[able] not to be bound to any other law than their old laws, which had been of long time continued and no fault found with them. Also Vilandry brought forth two new proclamations which for things to come were very profitable for England, for which he had a letter of thanks to the King his master. He required also pardon and releasement of imprisonment for certain Frenchmen taken on the seacoast. It was shown him [that] they were pirates, how some of them should by justice be punished, some by clemency pardoned; and with this dispatch he departed.

10. Removing to Westminster.

11. Horne, Dean of Durham, declared a secret conspiracy of the Earl of Westmoreland [in] the year of the apprehension of the Duke of Somerset – how he would have taken out treasure at Middleham and would have robbed his mother and sold £200 [of] land and, to please the people, would have made a proclamation for the bringing up of the coin, because he saw them grudge at the fall. He was commanded to keep this matter close.

6. Mr. Morrison, ambassador with the Emperor, declared to the Emperor the matter of the Turks before specified; whose answer was, he thanked us for our gentle offer and would cause the Regent to send a man for the same purpose to know our further meaning in that behalf.

11. Mr. Pickering declared to the French King, being then at Reims, Stuckley's matter, confession, and the cause of his imprisonment; who, after protestation made of his own good meaning in the amity and of Stuckley's ingratitude toward him, lewdness, and ill demeanour, thanked us much for this so gentle an uttering of the matter, that we would not be led with false bruits and tales.

15. The Bishop Tunstall of Durham was deprived of his bishopric. In this month Mons. de Rie, Martin [van] Rossem, and an army of

Flemings (while the French [King] had assembled his men of war in Lorraine, had sent the Constable to the army which lay four leagues from Verdun, the Duke of Guise with 7,000 men to Metz, and the Maréchal St. André to Verdun) razed and [de]spoiled between the river of Somme and Oise many towns and villages, as Noyon, Roye, Chauny, Nesles, Folembray, a new[ly] built house of the King's, etc., insomuch that the French King sent the Admiral of France to help the Duke of Vendôme against that army. There was at this time that reigned a great plague in sundry parts of France, of which many men died.

20. A man of the Earl of Tyrone's was committed to the Tower because he had made an untrue suggestion and complaint against the Deputy and the whole Council of Ireland. Also he had bruited certain ill bruits in Ireland, how the Duke of Northumberland and the Earl of Pembroke were fallen out, and one against another in the field.

17. The Flemings, and the Englishmen that took their parts, assaulted by night Hamleteu; the Englishmen were on the walls, and some of the Flemings also, but by the cowardice of great part of the Flemings the enterprise was lost and many men slain. The number of the Flemings was 4,000; the number of the men within Hamleteu, 400. The captain of this enterprise was Mons. de Vendeville, Captain of Gravelines.

6. Mons. de Bossu entered Trèves with a Flemish army to the number of 12,000 footmen and 2,500 horsemen Burgundians, without any resistance, because the ensigns there left by Marquis Albert were departed, and thereupon the Duke of Alva and the Marquis of Marignano marched[?] toward Metz; the Emperor himself and the Marquis Hans of Brandenburg, having with him the rest of his army, the 9th day of this month departed from Landau toward Metz. Monsieur de Bossu his army also joined with him at a place called Zweibrücken or Deuxponts.

23. It was agreed that, because the state of Ireland could not be known without the Deputy's presence, that he should in this dead time of the year leave the governance of the realm to the Council there for the time

and bring with him the whole estate of the realm, whereby such order might be taken as the superfluous charge might be avoided, and also the realm kept in quietness and the revenue of the land better and more profitably gathered.

25. Whereas one George Paris, Irishman, who had been a practiser between the Earl of Desmond and other Irish Lords and the French King, did now, being weary of that matter, practise means to come home and to have his old lands in Ireland again; his pardon was granted him and a letter written to him from my Council in which he was promised to be considered and helped.

There fell in this month a great contention among the Scots. For the Carrs slew the Lord of Buccleuch in a fray in Edinburgh, and as soon as they had done, they associated to them the Lord Home and all his kin. But the Governor thereupon summoned (his *crossed out*) an army to go against them. But at length, because the Dowager of Scotland favoured the Carrs and Homes, and so did all the French faction – the French King also having sent for 5,000 Scottish footmen and 500 horsemen for his aid in these wars – the Governor agreed [that] the 5,000 footmen under the leading of the Earl of Cassilis, and 500 light horsemen, of which the Carrs and Homes should be captains, should go with such haste into France that they might be in such place as the French King would point them to serve in by Christmas, or Candlemas [February 2] at the furtherest. And thus he trusted to be well rid of his most mortal enemies.

27. The Scots, hearing that George Paris practised for pardon, committed him to ward in Stirling Castle.

25. Mons. de Rie, having burned in France eighteen leagues in length and three leagues in breadth, having burned, pill[ag]ed, sacked, and razed the fair towns of Noyon, Roye, Nesles, and Chauny, the king's new house of Folembray, and infinite other villages, bulwarks, and gentlemen's houses in Champagne and Picardy, returned into Flanders.

23. The Emperor in his person came to the town of Metz with his army, which was reckoned 45,000 footmen, as the bruit went, and 7,000 horsemen. The Duke of Alva with a good band went to view the town, upon whom issued out the soldiers of the town and slew of his men about 2,000 and kept him [in] play till the main force of the camp came down, which caused them to retire with loss. On the French party was the Duke of Nemours hurt on the thigh. There was in the town as captain the Duke of Guise, and there were many other great lords with him, as the Prince of Roche-sur-Yon, the Duke of Nemours, the Vidame of Chartres, Pietro Strozzi, Mons. Châtillon, and many other gentlemen.

NOVEMBER

5. Mons. de Villandry returned to declare how the King his master did again offer to deliver four ships against which judgment had [been] passed. He said the King would appoint men to hear our merchants at Paris, which should be men of the best sort. He said likewise how the King his master meant to amend the ordinance, of which amendments he had brought articles.

7. These articles were delivered to be considered by the Secretaries.

9. Certain [men] were thought to be sought out by several commissions, viz., whether I was justly answered of the plate, lead, iron, etc., that belonged to [the] abbeys; whether I was justly answered [of] the profit of alum, copper, fustians, etc., which were [ap]pointed to be sold; and suchlike articles.

12. Mons. Villandry received answer for the first article as he died before: how I meant not by taking freely so few to prejudice the rest. For hearing of our merchants' matters at Paris by an inferior council we thought both too dilatory after these long suits and also unreasonable, because the inferior council could undo nothing (though cause appeared) which had been before judges by the higher council. And as for the new ordinances, we liked [them] in effect as ill as their old and desired none other but the old accustomed which have been used in France of late

time and be yet continued between England and the Low Country. Finally, we desired no more words, but deeds.

4. The Duke d'Aumale, being left in Lorraine – both to stop the Emperor's provision, to annoy his camp, and to take up the stragglers of the army – with a band of 400 men of arms, which is 1,200 horse and 800 light horse, hearing how Marquis Albert [of Brandenburg] began to take the Emperor's part, sent first certain light horse to view what they [could]. Those vauntcouriers lighted on a troop of 500 horsemen, who drove them back till they came to the Duke's person. Whereupon the skirmish grew so great that the Marquis, with 12,000 footmen and 1,000 horsemen, came to his men's succour, and so the Duke's part was discomfited, the Duke himself taken, and hurt in many places. Mons. de Rohan was also slain, and many other gentlemen slain and taken. This fight was before Toul, into which fort escaped a great part of the light horse.

6. Hesdin [Heding *in manuscript*] town and castle was taken by Mons, de Rie. The castle was reckoned too well stored of all things and rendered either by cowardice or treason. The battery was very small and not suitable. The most was that the captain, Mons. Genlis, was with one of the first shots of the cannon slain, and his lieutenant with him. In this month Fernando [di] Gonzaga besieged St. Martin's in Piedmont.

18, There was a commission granted out to Sir Richard Cotton, Sir John Gates, Sir Robert Bowes, and Sir Walter Mildmay, to examine the account of fall of money by the two proclamations.

20. The Lord Ogle leaving the wardenship of the Middle Marches, because my Lord Evre's land lay there, he [Lord Evre] was made Deputy Warden there with the fee of 600 marks, and Sir Thomas Dacre of the East Marches[17] with the fee of 500 marks.

---

[17] This is incorrect. It should read 'West Marches'.

24. Thomas Gresham came from Antwerp hither to declare how Mons. de Longin, treasurer to the Emperor of Flanders, was sent to him from the Regent with a certain packet of letters which the Burgundians had taken in Boulognois [country], coming from the Dowager of Scotland, the effect whereof was how she had committed George Paris, the Irishman, to prison because she had heard of his meaning to return into England; how she had found the pardon he had, and divers other writings; and how she had sent O'Connor's son into Ireland to comfort the Lords of Ireland. Also he showed certain instructions, a 1548, upon the Admiral's fall, given to a gentleman that came hither, that if there were any heir of the Admiral's faction he should do his utmost to raise an uproar.

29. Harry [Sir Francis] Knollys was sent in post into Ireland with a letter to stay the Deputy if he met him in Ireland, because of this business, and that he should seem to stay for his own affairs and prolong his going from week to week, lest it be perceived. Also he had with him certain articles concerning the whole state of the realm, which the Deputy was willed to answer.

30. There was a letter of thanks written to the Regent and sent to Mr. Chamberlain to deliver [to] her, for the gentle overture made to Thomas Gresham by the treasurer Longin. He was also willed to use gentle words in the delivery of the letters, wishing a further amity; and for recompense of her overture, to tell her of the French King's practise for 5,000 Scottish footmen and 500 horsemen, and also how he takes up by exchange at Lübeck an £100,000, whereby appears some meaning that way, the next spring.

28. The Lord Paget was put to his fine of £6,000, and £2,000 diminished, to pay it within the space of [*blank*] years at days limited.[18]

---

[18] Edward's *Chronicle* comes to an abrupt end. Little more than six months later, in July 1553, he would be dead.

Glossary

Accite: to call or send for officially or by authority.

Affrayed: frightened

Almain: German

Bards: trappings for the forequarters of a horse.

Barriers: lists

Bruits: rumours

Cast: convicted

Curtal: a horse with a docked tail.

Divers: several

Doubles: a duplicate

Double quartan: a periodic ague or fever.

Ensigns: troops or companies.

Gest: the various stages of a journey (particularly that of a royal progress).

Guidon: pennant

Incontinent: immediately

Jennet: a small and highly sought-after Spanish horse.

Lucre: profit

Mansions: houses or tents

Mean: mediator

Or ere: before ever

Organs: firearms or cannon (especially elaborate ones).

Osmunds: bars of high quality iron, imported from the Baltic; suitable for the manufacture of objects such as arrow-heads and fish-hooks.

Practice: conspiracy or treachery

Quit cost: be a return for or 'balance'.

Rascals: the rank and file of an army.

Reciproque: 'the like'

Rehearsed: cited or quoted

Rempared: fortified

Rovers: (in archery) shooting at a randomly selected target from an unfixed distance.

Scantling: a small amount.

Scour: to command an area with one's guns.

Sewer: an attendant responsible for supervising the ceremonial aspects of dining.

Slaughterhouse: a heavily armed and fortified strong point.

Spial: to spy, observe or watch.

Tainted: hit

Taints: broken lances

Vaunt-couriers: scouts

Vent: a market for commodities.

Key Figures

Sir John and Sir Thomas Arundell were brothers from a wealthy Cornish family. Though not directly involved in the Prayer Book Rebellion (1549), they hailed from a religiously conservative family and were watched closely by the authorities in its aftermath. Sir Thomas's luck ran out in 1552 when he was executed for his connections with the deposed Protector, Edward Seymour. Sir John, who served as Sheriff of Cornwall on two separate occasions, avoided this fate and died in 1557.

Thomas Atwood was a military engineer, most notable for his work in Alderney, Guernsey and Scilly.

Sir John Baker (c. 1488-1558) served as Chancellor of the Exchequer under Henry VIII, Edward VI and Mary I, as well as being a Privy Councillor and occupying the prestigious post of Speaker of the House of Commons. He is best remembered as 'Bloody Baker' – a fierce persecutor of Protestants.

Daniel Barbaro (1514-1570) was an Italian architect and politician. As well as being elected to the ecclesiastical post of Patriarch of Aquileia, he was a representative at the Council of Trent and served as the Republic of Venice's ambassador to Edward VI's court.

John, Earl of Bedford (c. 1485-1555) benefitted handsomely from the Dissolution of the Monasteries and held a number of high offices in government, including Lord High Admiral and Lord Privy Seal. He also had the honour of being Lord High Steward for Edward VI's coronation.

Sir Edward Bellingham (c. 1506-1549) was an experienced soldier, Member of Parliament and short-lived but successful Lord Deputy of Ireland from 1548-49.

John Belmaine was a French Huguenot and humanist scholar. Due to the persecution of Protestants in his native France, he fled to England where he served as the French-language tutor to the future Edward VI and Elizabeth I. It is possible that he played a key role in developing the Protestant views of both monarchs.

Berteville was a French mercenary and adventurer. He fought for the English over a long period of time, including at the Battle of Pinkie (1547), while at the same time passing news and information onto the French ambassador in London.

Joan Bocher (or Boucher) was an Anabaptist who was burned at the stake in 1550 for heresy. It was the first religious execution of Edward VI's reign.

Sir John Borthwick served as an English representative to the Baltic countries for part of Edward VI's reign.

Sir Robert Bowes (c. 1495-1554) was a soldier and lawyer who became a trusted expert on affairs in the Scottish Marches.

John, Margrave of Brandenburg-Küstrin (1513-1571) was a deeply religious Protestant who nevertheless sided with the Catholic Holy Roman Emperor Charles V against the Schmalkaldic League. His relationship with the Emperor later soured when he received few rewards for his support.

Sir Edward Braye served in a range of political positions, including as a Member of Parliament, Lieutenant of Calais Castle, Constable of the Tower of London, and the High Sheriff of Surrey and Sussex. He was also a Justice of the Peace and captain in the Royal Navy.

George Brooke was a member of Edward VI's Privy Council who also served as Deputy of Calais from 1544 to 1549.

Sir Anthony Browne (c. 1500-1548) was an English courtier, most notable for being Master of the Horse.

Martin Bucer (1491-1551) was a German Protestant reformer. His efforts resulted in his excommunication from the Catholic Church, and he fled into exile in England. As well as being a mediator between the two most prominent reformers, Martin Luther and Huldrych Zwingli, it is highly likely that he influenced the second edition of the Book of Common Prayer.

Sir William Cecil (1520-1598) served as Edward VI's Principal Secretary, as well as Elizabeth I's chief advisor for much of her reign. He was twice Secretary of State (1550-53 and 1558-72) and Lord High Treasurer from 1572 until his death.

Sir Thomas Chaloner (c. 1521-1565) was an English statesman, diplomat and poet. In spite of his Protestant views, he continued to be employed by the government of Mary I after Edward VI's death.

Sir Thomas Chamberlain was the president of the guild of English merchants trading in Flanders and assisted the government in its attempts to smooth out the increasingly fractious Anglo-Flemish relationship.

Charles V, Holy Roman Emperor (1500-1558) was Holy Roman Emperor and Archduke of Austria from 1519 to 1556, King of Spain from 1516 to 1556, and Lord of the Netherlands as titular Duke of Burgundy from 1506 to 1555. At the time the most powerful man in Europe, Charles V revitalised the medieval concept of the universal monarchy and spent most of his life defending the integrity of the Holy Roman Empire from the Protestant Reformation, as well as the unbridled ambition of France and the Ottoman Empire. Ultimately, Charles V was forced to face up to reality and abandon his multi-national project. In a series of abdications in 1556, he split his domains between the Spanish Habsburgs (headed by his son, Philip II of Spain) and the Austrian Habsburgs (led by his brother, Ferdinand, who succeeded as Holy Roman Emperor).

John Cheke (c. 1514-1557) was Professor of Greek at Cambridge University and one of the most accomplished schoolmasters of his age.

He served as the future Edward VI's tutor and his Reformist sympathies are believed to have helped shape Edward's own religious beliefs.

Sir Thomas Cheyney (c. 1485-1558) was an English administrator and diplomat. He is perhaps most notable for being Lord Warden of the Cinque Ports from 1536 until his death.

Edward Clinton (c. 1512-1584/85) was an English landowner, peer and Lord High Admiral. Rendering valuable service to four successive Tudor monarchs, he was created Earl of Lincoln during the reign of Elizabeth I.

Lord John Conyers (c. 1524-1557) was an English military administrator. He was appointed Warden of the Western March and Governor of Calais under Edward VI, and Warden of the Eastern March and Governor of Berwick under Mary I.

Myles Coverdale (c. 1488-1569) was an English ecclesiastical reformer and preacher, best known for producing the first complete printed translation of the Bible into English. He briefly served as Bishop of Exeter between 1551 and 1553.

Richard Cox (c. 1500-1581) was a humanist reformer and clergyman who served as Dean of Westminster, Bishop of Ely and Chancellor of Oxford University. At the royal court, he was the future Edward VI's almoner and played a key role in the young prince's education.

Sir James Croft (c. 1518-1590) was a professional soldier, Member of Parliament and Lord Deputy of Ireland.

William Dacre (c. 1493-1563) was a soldier and peer who spent many years as Warden of the West Marches.

Sir Thomas Darcy (1506-1558) served as Vice-Chamberlain of the Household and Captain of the Yeomen of the Guard between 1550 and 1551 before becoming Lord Chamberlain of the Household. He was placed under house arrest for supporting Lady Jane Grey as Edward VI's successor.

Sir Maurice Dennis (or Denys) (c. 1516-1563) was an English lawyer and property speculator during the Dissolution of the Monasteries. He also served as a Member of Parliament and Treasurer of Calais.

Andrea Doria (1466-1560) was a Genoese statesman, condottiero and admiral, who is regarded as one of the most prominent naval leaders of his time.

Dragut (c. 1485-1565), also known as 'The Drawn Sword of Islam', was an Ottoman noble and naval commander. Under his watch, the Ottoman Empire expanded its maritime power across North Africa.

Sir Andrew Dudley (c. 1507-1559) was an English soldier, diplomat and courtier. A younger brother of John Dudley, Duke of Northumberland, he served in the navy and was appointed captain of the fortress of Guînes in the Pale of Calais in 1551. In political life, he was one of Edward VI's Chief Gentlemen of the Privy Chamber and later became responsible for the Royal Wardrobe and Privy Purse in his capacity as keeper of the Palace of Westminster.

Sir Henry Dudley was a professional solider and a distant relative of John Dudley, Duke of Northumberland. He was appointed captain of Guînes in 1551 and Vice-Admiral the following year.

John Dudley, Duke of Northumberland (c. 1504-1553) was an English politician and admiral who was *de facto* head of Edward VI's minority government from 1550 until 1553. He played an instrumental role in the downfall and execution of his predecessor, Edward Seymour, Duke of Somerset, and met the same fate after failing to install his daughter-in-law Lady Jane Grey as Edward VI's successor.

Sir John Dymoke was the third successive member of his family to serve as King's Champion. His more famous father, of the same name, had served in this capacity at the coronations of Richard III, Henry VII and Henry VIII.

Lady Elizabeth (1533-1603) was Edward VI's half-sister and would go on to rule as Queen from 1558 to her death. Sometimes called the 'Virgin Queen', 'Gloriana' or 'Good Queen Bess', Elizabeth was the last of the five monarchs of the House of Tudor, and saved Edward VI's Protestant legacy in the aftermath of the reign of his other half-sister, the arch-Catholic 'Bloody' Mary.

Thomas Erskine (d. 1551) was the heir apparent of John, Lord Erskine, but predeceased his father.

Henry Fitzalan, Earl of Arundel (c. 1512-1580) was an English nobleman who served as a Privy Councillor, Lord Chamberlain of the Household and Chancellor of Oxford University. A religious conservative, his influence came under threat during Edward VI's reign and he spent some time imprisoned in the Tower of London.

Barnaby Fitzpatrick (c.1535-1581) was the son of an Irish peer, who was sent to England during his childhood as an assurance of his father's loyalty to the Crown. Educated alongside the future Edward VI, he became the young king's most intimate friend. He completed his education at the French court and his life following Edward's death was primarily spent in Ireland, where he continued to be regarded as a loyal subject of the English monarchy.

Antoine Escalin des Aimars (c. 1516-1578) served as the French ambassador to the Ottoman Empire, as well as 'General of the galleys'.

Stephen Gardiner (c. 1483-1555) was Bishop of Winchester. His power and influence was significantly diminished during the Edwardian Reformation as a result of his conservative religious beliefs. He returned to royal favour upon Mary I's accession, being named Lord Chancellor.

Sir John Gates (c. 1504-1553) was a courtier and supporter of John Dudley, Earl of Northumberland. He was one of Edward VI's Chief Gentlemen of the Privy Chamber and was executed alongside Northumberland for his role in installing Lady Jane Grey on the throne.

Sir Jacques Granado was Esquire of the Stable to Edward VI.

Frances Grey, Duchess of Suffolk (1517-1559) was the eldest daughter of Charles Brandon, Duke of Suffolk and Henry VIII's younger sister, Princess Mary. She was the mother of the 'Nine Days' Queen', Lady Jane Grey.

Sir John Gresham (c. 1495-1556) was an English courtier, merchant and financier who served as Lord Mayor of London.

Sir William Grey (c. 1508-1562) was an English military commander, who served in wars in France and Scotland, as well as in the suppression of the Prayer Book Rebellion. He was also named commander of the fortress at Guînes.

Sir Edward Grimston (c. 1508-1600) was an English politician and comptroller of Calais.

Sir Anthony Guidotti was a London-based Florentine merchant who was frequently used by the Privy Council in informal but important diplomatic negotiations.

Francis, Duke of Guise (1519-1563) was a French general and politician. A prominent leader during the Italian War of 1551-59 and the French Wars of Religion, he was assassinated in 1563 during the siege of Orleans.

Gustav I (later known as Gustav Vasa) (c. 1496-1560) was King of Sweden from 1523 until his death in 1560. He gained the throne after deposing King Christian II of Denmark, Norway and Sweden during the Swedish War of Liberation.

Sir William Herbert (c. 1501-1570) was a courtier and politician who exercised considerable power during Edward VI's reign as one of the executors of Henry VIII's will. In 1551, he was created Earl of Pembroke.

Sir Philip Hoby (c. 1505-1558) served the Crown on a range of diplomatic missions, including as ambassador to Charles V, Holy Roman Emperor during Edward VI's reign.

John Hooper (c. 1495-1555) served briefly as the Bishop of Gloucester and Worcester during Edward VI's reign. As a vigorous supporter of the English Reformation, he was burned at the stake during the reign of Mary I.

Lord William Howard (c. 1510-1573) was an English diplomat and military leader. As well as being Lord Admiral and Lord Chamberlain of the Household, he served Henry VIII, Edward VI, Mary I and Elizabeth I in a range of official capacities, including on diplomatic missions.

Sir Andrew Judd (or Judde) was an English merchant and Lord Mayor of London.

Robert Kett (c. 1492-1549) was the leader and namesake of a major rebellion in 1549, centred on Norfolk. A moderately wealthy landowner, he is thought to have been a tanner by trade.

Sir Francis Knollys (d. 1596) was an English Member of Parliament and courtier in the service of Henry VIII, Edward VI and Elizabeth I.

Sir Richard Lee was a professional soldier and military engineer, and a long-time servant of the Tudor dynasty.

Charles de Marillac (c. 1510-1560) was a French diplomat who served as the French ambassador to England from 1539 to 1543.

Lady Mary (famously known as 'Bloody Mary') (1516-1588) was the half-sister of Edward VI. Despite Edward's attempts to rule her out of the line of succession, she became Queen after his death and immediately set about undoing his cherished Reformation of the Church. After Mary's death in 1558, her re-establishment of Roman Catholicism was in turn reversed by her younger half-sister and successor, Elizabeth I.

Mary, Queen of Scots (1542-87) assumed the Scottish throne as an infant and her failed betrothal to the future Edward VI triggered the 'Rough Wooing'. She married three times, including to Francis II of France, before she was forced to abdicate in 1567 (when Mary and her third husband James Hepburn were implicated with the murder of her second husband Henry Stuart). After fleeing into exile in England, she was imprisoned by Elizabeth I who regarded Mary as a threat to her crown. She was executed in 1587.

Sir John Mason (c. 1503-1566) was a diplomat of humble origins who was appointed as the English ambassador to France in 1550.

Sir Peter Meutas was an English courtier. He served as Governor of Guernsey and was part of the delegation sent to greet Anne of Cleves upon her arrival at Calais in 1540.

Sir Walter Mildmay was a politician who served as Chancellor of the Exchequer during the reign of Queen Elizabeth I.

Sir Richard Morison (c. 1513-1556) was an English humanist scholar and diplomat. A protégé of Thomas Cromwell, he served as the English ambassador to the Imperial court during the reign of Edward VI.

Sir Richard Musgrave (c. 1524-1555) was an English politician, Justice of the Peace and Member of Parliament. He held a range of offices in the late 1540s and early 1550s, including High Sheriff of Cumberland and Captain of Carlisle Castle.

Sir Henry Neville (c. 1520-1593) was a Gentleman of the Privy Chamber to King Henry VIII. Neville was closely aligned with John

Dudley, Duke of Northumberland, who promoted him to Gentleman of the Privy chamber during the reign of Edward VI.

Murrough O'Brien, Earl of Thomond (d. 1551) was the last King of Thomond, and a descendant of the 11th century High King of Ireland, Brian Boru.

Thomas Butler, Earl of Ormond and Earl of Ossory (c. 1531-1614) was an influential courtier during the reign of Elizabeth I. He was knighted at Edward VI's coronation and served as Lord Treasurer of Ireland from 1559 to his death.

William Paget (c. 1506-1563) was an English politician and accountant who held a number of prominent positions during the reigns of Henry VIII, Edward VI and Mary I. In 1547 he was elected as a Member of Parliament, made a knight of the Garter, and appointed controller of the king's household and Chancellor of the Duchy of Lancaster. He was briefly imprisoned in the Tower of London following the fall of Somerset's protectorate and retired from public life on the accession of Elizabeth I.

Sir Harry Palmer (d. 1553) was an English soldier and courtier, whose testimony was crucial in the final downfall of Edward Seymour, Duke of Somerset. Little over a year later Palmer himself was executed for his support of Lady Jane Grey in the succession crisis of 1553.

William Parr, Marquess of Northampton (c. 1513-1571) was the only brother of Henry VIII's sixth and final wife, Catherine Parr. As a prominent member of the Protestant faction at the royal court, he enjoyed the favour of Henry VIII, Edward VI and Elizabeth I.

Sir Miles Partridge (d. 1552) was an English courtier and soldier, who acquired fame for his skill and valour at the Battle of Pinkie (1547). An ally of Edward Seymour, Duke of Somerset, he was hanged for treason in the aftermath of the fall of the Protectorship.

Thomas Petitt was a military engineer, best known for being in charge of Calais' elaborate defences throughout the reign of Edward VI.

Sir William Petre (pronounced Peter) (c. 1505-1572) was an English lawyer and politician who served as Secretary of State under Henry VIII, Edward VI and Mary I. He probably owed his rise to the corridors of power to the family of Henry VIII's second wife, Anne Boleyn; having served as tutor to Anne's brother, George, at Oxford.

Sir William Pickering (c. 1516-1575) was a courtier and diplomat who was appointed as England's ambassador to France in 1551. He was recalled sometime after the accession of Mary I.

John Ponet (or Poynet) (c. 1514-1556) was a Protestant clergyman and controversial writer. As well as being Bishop of Winchester and a Marian exile, he was well-known for his attack on the divine right of kings.

Pallavicino Rangone was a young Italian nobleman who spent some time in Edward VI's personal service, for which he was richly rewarded. When his cousin was killed in 1551, he became the heir of his uncle, Count Guido Rangone.

Richard Rich (c. 1496-1567) was Lord Chancellor during Edward VI's reign, from 1547 until January 1552. He had previously served as Speaker of the House of Commons and was a beneficiary of the Dissolution of the Monasteries – persecuting opponents of the reformed church and state.

Nicholas Ridley (c. 1500-1555) was an English clergyman who served as Bishop of London and Westminster. One of the 'Oxford Martyrs', he was burned at the stake during the Marian Persecutions for his Protestant beliefs and his support of Lady Jane Grey.

Sir Edward Rogers (c. 1498-1567) was a skilled Crown official and beneficiary of the Dissolution of the Monasteries. After being made one of Edward VI's Gentlemen of the Privy Chamber in 1549, he was briefly imprisoned for suspected connections to the then out-of-favour Earl of Arundel. He reached the peak of his power during the reign of Elizabeth I, when he became Comptroller and Vice-Chamberlain of the Household.

John Rogers was a military engineer, whose postings included Boulogne, Guernsey and Ireland.

John Rogers (c. 1505-1555) was an English clergyman, Bible translator and commentator. He was the first Protestant martyr of Mary I's short but bloody reign.

Martin van Rossem (or Maarten van Rossum) (c. 1478-1555) was a military tactician who served as field marshal to Charles, Duke of Guelders. He was greatly feared by soldiers and civilians alike for his ruthless guerrilla tactics, highlighted by his motto: *'Blaken en branden is het sieraad van de oorlog'* ('Burning and torching is the jewel of war').

Sir Ralph Sadler (c. 1507-1587) was an English politician, who served Henry VIII as a Privy Councillor, Secretary of State and ambassador to Scotland. He continued to provide services to the Crown under Edward VI and Elizabeth I, and was appointed Chancellor of the Duchy of Lancaster during the latter reign.

Cornelius de Schepper (also known by his Latin name Scepperus) (c. 1503-1555) was a Flemish counsellor, who served the Holy Roman Emperors Charles V and Ferdinand I, and Mary of Hungary, as an ambassador.

Edward Seymour, Duke of Somerset (c. 1500-1552) was the eldest surviving brother of Henry VIII's third wife, Jane Seymour. He was Lord Protector of England from 1547 to 1549 during the minority of his nephew Edward VI. Despite his popularity with the common people, his policies often angered the gentry and he was overthrown by his fellow councillors.

Jane Seymour (c. 1508-1537) was Queen of England from 1536 to 1537 as Henry VIII's third wife. She died from postnatal complications a matter of days after the birth of her only child – the future Edward VI.

Thomas Seymour (c. 1508-1549) was the younger brother of the Lord Protector of England, Edward Seymour, Duke of Somerset. An ambitious and power-hungry man, he vied with his sibling for control of their young nephew, Edward VI. He was executed in 1549 following a failed attempt to kidnap the king.

Sir William Sharington was an English courtier, Member of Parliament and High Sheriff of Wiltshire. He was an ally of Thomas Seymour and was found guilty of embezzlement while serving as master of the Bristol Mint.

Edmund Sheffield was created Baron Sheffield in 1547 and was killed fighting under the command of the Marquis of Northampton during the Norfolk rising of 1549.

Sir Henry Sidney (c. 1529-1586) was the eldest son of the prominent courtier Sir William Sidney of Penshurst and was raised at the royal court as a companion of the future Edward VI. He continued to enjoy royal favour under Mary and Elizabeth I, and served as Lord Deputy of Ireland three times.

Sir Clement Smith (c. 1515-1552) was a Member of Parliament who also served as Lord Treasurer's Remembrancer in the Exchequer (often erroneously called 'Chief Baron of the Exchequer').

Sir Richard Southwell (c. 1502-1564) was an English Privy Councillor.

Jacques d'Albon, Seigneur de Saint-André (c. 1505-1562) was a French soldier and favourite of Henri II of France. He was made marshal of France, governor of Lyonnais and ambassador to England.

Sir Anthony St. Leger (c. 1496-1559) was an agent of Thomas Cromwell who served as Lord Deputy of Ireland.

Sir Thomas Stradling was a Welsh politician and Member of Parliament.

Robert Stewart, Earl of Orkney and Lord of Zetland (Shetland) (c. 1533-1593) was a recognised illegitimate son of James V of Scotland, as well as the half-brother of Mary, Queen of Scots.

Thomas Stuckley (c. 1520-1578) was a mercenary and adventurer, thought by many of his contemporaries to be an illegitimate son of Henry VIII. Working as a soldier and agent for both the English and French, his services always went to the highest bidder. He spent some time imprisoned in the Tower of London during Edward VI's reign and was killed fighting against the Moors at the Battle of Alcazar (1578).

Thomas Thirlby (or Thirleby) (c. 1506-1570) was the first and only Bishop of Westminster (1540–50), and later served as Bishop of Norwich (1550-54) and Bishop of Ely (1554-59). Although he acquiesced with Henry VIII's break with Rome, he otherwise remained loyal to traditional Catholic doctrine during the English Reformation.

William Thomas (d. 1554) was a Welsh scholar of Italian language and history, as well as a clerk of the Privy Council under Edward VI. He was executed for treason during the reign of Mary I, in the aftermath of Wyatt's Rebellion.

Sir Nicholas Throckmorton (c. 1515-1571) was a diplomat and Member of Parliament, who served as the English ambassador to France and Scotland. He played a key role in the relationship between Elizabeth I of England and Mary, Queen of Scots and held the post of under-treasurer at the Tower mint from 1549 to 1552.

Captain Francisco Tiberio was the commander of an Italian mercenary troop and spent a number of years in English service.

Lazarus Tucker was a prominent banker based in Antwerp. He secured a loan of £10,000 for Edward VI's cash-strapped government in 1552, and his financial relations with the English government continued into the reign of Mary I.

Peter Vannes was an Italian clergyman and diplomat who served both Henry VIII and Edward VI as Latin Secretary. He was also Dean of Salisbury and represented England in the Republic of Venice from 1550 to 1556.

François de Vendôme, Vidame de Chartres (c. 1522-1560) was a French soldier and courtier who was sent to England in 1549 as one of the French hostages in connection with the Treaty of Boulogne. According to reports, he became extraordinarily popular at the English court.

Sir John Wallop (c. 1490-1551) was an English soldier and diplomat who served as captain of Guînes.

Nicholas Wotton (c. 1497-1567) was an English diplomat, cleric and Member of Parliament.

Sir John Williams (c. 1500-1559) was Master of the Jewels, Treasurer of the Court of Augmentations and Lord President of the Council of the Welsh Marches. In the first two positions, he was imprisoned during the reign of Edward VI following an audit of his accounts. He returned to favour during the reigns of Mary I and Elizabeth I.

Sir Hugh Willoughby (d. 1554) was an English soldier and explorer. In 1533, he led a fleet of three vessels – sponsored by a company of London merchants – to search for a new route to the Far East via the Northeast Passage. Willoughby died along with the crews of two of the ships, while the third vessel went on to establish a successful and long-lasting trading relationship with Russia.

Sir Anthony Wingfield (d. 1552) was an English soldier, politician, courtier and Member of Parliament. He was the Lord Lieutenant of

Suffolk and Vice-Chamberlain of the Household during the reign of Edward VI.

William Winter (or Wynter) was an English merchant who traded primarily with the Levant. He also worked for the English Crown as Surveyor of Ships.

Thomas Wriothesley, Earl of Southampton (1505-1550) was an English politician who served as Secretary of State, Lord Chancellor and Lord High Admiral. He remained loyal to Henry VIII during his break with the Catholic Church, but sided with the conservative faction upon the accession of Edward VI.

Sir John York (c. 1490-1569) was an English merchant, landowner and Member of Parliament who became Master of the Mint.

To find out more about the extraordinary life and times of Edward VI, why not try...

Edward VI: England's Boy King by B.R. Egginton

Printed in Great Britain
by Amazon